"Consultant Sher, formerly the longtime CEO of a midsized company, worries about the state of the American midsized firms. As the founder of CEO to CEO, Inc., he works with business leaders to help medium-sized companies grow and expand. This primer is aimed at the leaders of midsized companies, which make up a significant portion of the American economy; there are nearly 200,000 companies with revenues between $10 million and $1 billion, some privately or family-held, and some publicly funded. Problems specific to mid sized companies are not always visible or widely discussed in M.B.A. courses or the media, he argues. These companies struggle with low tolerance for risk, few ways to develop talent, less strategic thinking, and less seasoned talent. The titular seven silent killers are letting time slip-slide away; strategy tinkering at the top; reckless attempts at growth; fumbled strategic acquisitions; operational meltdown; the liquidity crash; and tolerating dysfunctional leaders. Using numerous case studies and presenting thorough plans for overcoming each of the silent killers, Sher writes passionately about the ways in which leaders can become aware of these challenges and rally their management teams. This is a quiet but hard-hitting game plan." —*Publishers Weekly*

"Robert Sher has written a very important book in these times of economic uncertainty, and every executive team member of a midsized company should read it. *Mighty Midsized Companies* will help them do the right thing, which is what I've long said is what truly distinguishes leaders from managers."
—Warren Bennis, author and Distinguished
Professor of Business Administration at the
University of Southern California

"Through interviews with CEOs as well as real-life case studies, author Robert Sher shows readers how to keep a midsized company healthy and avoid the seven dangerous mistakes that kill growth. *Mighty Midsized Companies* is a must-read guide to ensure your organization remains strong and viable."

—Ken Blanchard, coauthor of
The One Minute Manager® and
Legendary Service

"Robert Sher offers powerful insights into how to address the critical issues that can derail growth in midsized companies."

—Douglas Conant, former CEO, Campbell
Soup Company, and the *New York Times*
best-selling author of *TouchPoints*

"At a time when midsized organizations desperately struggle to keep pace in a global economy, Robert Sher provides real-world insight into the pitfalls that prevent growth. *Mighty Midsized Companies* superbly identifies the seven silent killers that routinely throw a wrench into a company's development and provides excellent solutions for fostering success. A terrific read."

—Stephen M. R. Covey, author of the
New York Times and *Wall Street Journal* best seller
The Speed of Trust and coauthor of *Smart Trust*

"What a valuable book! Rob Sher understands the unique opportunities—and temptations—that middle market companies meet on their road to growth. *Mighty Midsized Companies* is a useful guide and wise companion for the journey."

—Thomas A. Stewart, executive director,
National Center for the Middle Market

"This is it, the next frontier in management thinking—to understand the unique challenges that face leaders of midsized companies. And not a moment too soon. These companies have been bailing out the U.S. economy for more than a decade now, while the rest of the economy is stalled when it comes to the level of job creation we need to keep the economy healthy and robust. Robert Sher's insightful and useful book could only have been created by someone who's been immersed in this world as practitioner and thought leader. Let's hope that this book is the first of many to shine the spotlight of public attention on this high-performing sector and its leaders."

—George Gendron, long-time editor-in-chief of *Inc. Magazine* and founder of The Build Network for midsized companies, a co-venture of *Inc. Magazine* and *Fast Company*

MIGHTY
MIDSIZED
COMPANIES

MIGHTY MIDSIZED

COMPANIES

HOW LEADERS OVERCOME
7 SILENT GROWTH KILLERS

ROBERT SHER

bibliomotion
books + media

First published by Bibliomotion, Inc.
39 Harvard Street
Brookline, MA 02445
Tel: 617-934-2427

www.bibliomotion.com

Printed in the United States of America

Library of Congress Cataloging-in-Publication Data

Sher, Robert, 1961–
    Mighty midsized companies : how leaders overcome 7 silent growth killers / Robert Sher.
        pages cm
    Summary: "Drawing upon his own experience and interviews with more than 100 companies, author Robert Sher runs through seven "silent growth killers" that plague midsized companies and which, if not addressed, eventually cripple growth. Mighty Midsized Companies offers clear, tangible, actionable advice about dealing with these killers and growing despite them"— Provided by publisher.
    ISBN 978-1-62956-006-9 (hardback) — ISBN 978-1-62956-007-6 (ebook) — ISBN 978-1-62956-008-3 (enhanced ebook)
    1. Small business—Management. 2. Small business—Growth. 3. Leadership. I. Title.
    HD62.7.S52575 2014
    658.4'06—dc23
                                                    2014013350

*To the leaders of midsized businesses everywhere,
who despite all the challenges, get up every day
and strive to build mighty midsized companies.*

CONTENTS

FOREWORD

by Jim Horan

Author of *The One Page Business Plan*

Nearly twenty years ago, when I began writing my first book on how to create one-page business plans, I had an inkling the book might do very well—even if I couldn't get a publishing house behind it. In 1994, four years after I had left the big-company world, I gave five public presentations on my idea—that the best business plans were short yet cogent. The following year, I was asked to do fifteen speeches, and my audiences began asking for the book version of the idea. In my mind, some of the "asking" bordered on "demanding."

So when my self-published book hit the market in 1997, I was delighted to see it flying off the virtual book shelves of Amazon.com. It became an Amazon bestseller and spawned five related books, which collectively have sold nearly 100,000 copies and been translated into four languages.

But, again, I wasn't totally surprised, having sensed my conference audiences' burning interest in the concept well before my first book came out. I had a strong hunch it would do well.

I have the same feeling about *Mighty Midsized Companies*, and here's why. Robert Sher is the preeminent thought leader on midsized businesses. I have known and observed Robert as a business owner, facilitator of a networking group for CEOs, public speaker, and private confidant to my firm. He understands the midsized company because he has lived it. He sees through the noise that distracts us all and goes straight to the underlying causes. His ability to do this is uncanny!

One of the many things I love about this book is that Robert eloquently articulates what goes unarticulated, and therefore unaddressed, in the hundreds of midsized firms I have come to know. As an example of this rare skill to memorably explain the previously inexplicable, Robert gives simple but provocative names to the issues that kill the growth of these firms. When he talks about letting time slip slide away, tinkering with strategy, reckless attempts at growth, fumbled strategic acquisitions, operational meltdowns, liquidity crashes and tolerating dysfunctional leaders, Robert is speaking to you and me!

A tremendous amount of research went into this book. Robert weaves in numerous case studies that illustrate the power and danger of these silent killers. He describes how these killers fester and grow, and how CEOs and their teams successfully and unsuccessfully have dealt with them. Robert also gives very clear, actionable advice for keeping these silent killers at bay.

I believe every management team at the top of a midsized company could benefit greatly by learning these lessons. That is why I will be giving all my clients a copy of this book. And I will make sure my management team reads and embraces it as well.

Midsized companies buried within the corporate structure of multibillion-dollar firms could benefit equally from this book as well. I should know! In the first half of my career, I was a controller and CFO in midsized divisions of two companies: a multinational pharmaceutical firm (Bayer) and a consumer products company (Shaklee). It was in those two companies where I learned that the silent killers of growth and profitability are everywhere—even if I didn't have Robert's labels for the maladies or the cures that you will read in this book. As a young manager, then executive, I saw very few leaders who knew where and how these silent killers were bred. I knew even fewer who could effectively kill them.

Life is likely to only get harder for executives running midsized companies over the rest of the decade and beyond. Global competition, technological disruption of markets, and customers that continuously must do more with less will continue to force midsized companies to raise their game.

The next level of growth and success for your business is directly tied to the next level of discipline in how you and your team think about and prepare for growth. It is also about the discipline of tracking what is happening inside your company as well as in the surrounding world. This has been my mantra to midsized business leaders for over twenty years. In this book, Robert brings a whole new level of insight to this mantra.

You have hopes, dreams, and concerns. I urge you to use this book to educate yourself and your management team on the silent growth killers. It a practical, no-nonsense handbook that will trigger important insights and frank dialogue.

If you allow it to be, this book can be a catalyst for eliminating the silent growth killers lurking in your firm. They are preventable, and you need to do your best to prevent them!

If you do, I can't imagine anything will stop you from executing a well-crafted (and short) business plan and growing your firm reliably and profitably, year after year.

ACKNOWLEDGMENTS

I am grateful to many who helped me through years of research culminating in this beautiful book.

My thanks to the hundreds of company leaders who shared their stories, both sad and glad, with an openness that allowed me to probe the depths of the seven silent growth killers. I found those companies with the help of the Alliance of Chief Executives (staff and members), my peers at the Association for Corporate Growth—San Francisco, and the Saint Mary's Graduate School of Business, as well as many others who made connections for me. Be sure to review the list of business leaders in the Appendix who gave their time in interviews over the past several years.

I must especially thank all my clients, whose challenges and wisdom have taught me much and contributed hugely to this book. A special thanks to Bob Buday of the Bloom Group, my guide to stepping up my game as a thought leader, who contributed in many powerful ways to the creation of the book.

During the research phase I had much support. My assistant, Jan Dare Brown scheduled countless interviews and generally kept me on track. She also managed the enormous flow of work as all the interviews were summarized, reviewed, studied, and excerpts approved. It takes a lot to pull the key lessons out of thousands of pages of interview transcripts. My thanks in the interviewing and interview analysis process to Warren Lutz, David Wagstaff, Chris Benjamin, and Tom Thurber.

David Rosenbaum and Bob Buday both acted as my editors, giving me excellent feedback and counsel as the manuscript developed. It never ceases to amaze me that even when I do my best writing, they can still make it better.

When the manuscript seemed finished, I asked four deeply experienced midsized business executives to read it critically, and their feedback resulted in quite a number of improvements. I am grateful to Jerry Turin, David Dutton, Dave Weil, and Michael Law.

Thank you to my agent Joelle Delbourgo who found the superior team at Bibliomotion, my publisher, as well as to my illustrator, Cristian Enache.

Thank you to our research participants. We are very grateful to all those who participated in our research. For a full listing of research participants, please see the Appendix.

Most important are my wife Renee and our two children Ben and Jessie, who even after my first book, still encouraged me to research and write another, which meant they saw less of me, rather than more.

INTRODUCTION

Midsized firms are the foundation of the American economy. There are almost two hundred thousand companies today with revenues between $10 million and $1 billion—midsized, as defined by Ohio State University's Fisher College of Business—and they account for about a third of U.S. GDP and a third of all U.S. jobs.[1]

This book is for the leaders of these companies, businesses that don't get nearly the attention accorded their smaller and larger brethren even though they share equally severe headaches. Like all businesses, midsized companies struggle to innovate. They suffer defects in quality that turn off customers and lead to expensive recalls. They fumble when it comes to entering new markets. They make dangerous and profound strategic and operational mistakes.

But midsized companies are different in important ways. They face unique challenges that smaller (less than $10 million in revenue) and bigger firms (more than $1 billion) do not experience. And the difficulties that uniquely confront midsized companies are often subtle...at least in the beginning.

Unlike dry spells in innovation, quality defects, and mistakes made in entering new markets, many of the problems that midsized companies must deal with (and the ones that I will explore in this book) are not obvious. They are not studied in business schools. They are not written about in the pages of the *Wall Street Journal*, the *Financial Times*, the business pages of your local paper, or in the trade press. Consultants don't specialize in them, and they don't write white papers about them.

These problems grow out of sight (and frequently out of mind) in the dark recesses of the midsized organization, unrecognized by management in their daily routines until they emerge as full-blown crises that can threaten the present and future of the businesses. As a result, I refer to these special afflictions of midsized companies—seven in all—as silent growth killers.

I believe silent growth killers is an appropriate name for them because they sneak up on leaders at midsized companies just as high blood pressure and high cholesterol can creep up on us, often unnoticed, and later cause multiple and massive complications. Just as those medical conditions, untreated, can lead to an early demise, these silent growth killers, if not addressed, may cause a businesses to collapse in a dysfunctional heap. But as I'll point out in subsequent chapters, many midsized companies have dealt with them well, and by doing so have grown nicely, profitably, and sometimes spectacularly. They have achieved mighty midsized company status.

Why This Book Is for You

The midsized firms that you will read about in this book are sandwiched between two ends of the revenue spectrum. On one end, we find millions of small companies, a highly heterogeneous group ranging from the Main Street bakery to the Silicon Valley start-up. On the other end are the big companies, the billion-dollar corporations featured on the covers of *Fortune, Forbes,* and *Bloomberg Businessweek,* and often on the listings of the public stock exchanges.

This book is not for the men and women running the Main Street businesses with one or two employees, bringing home their profits to put food on their tables, nor for the highly compensated ivory tower executives captaining giant conglomerates. It is for executives and managers leading midsized firms, most privately held (often by families), and some externally funded (often by private equity firms, venture capital, or smaller publicly held firms). And some are professional services firms—law, accounting, consulting, IT services, training, and other firms—owned by the partners of those businesses.

You see, it is much more rewarding and comfortable to lead a mighty midsized company where there is less vulnerability to a host of problems that slow growth and destroy profit. So let's make your firm mighty.

It is also for those leaders whose companies are knocking on the midsized door with between $5 million and $10 million in revenue. There are 370,000 businesses of that size in the United States today. My advice applies to their managers as well because as they grow to middlehood they are sure to encounter the issues I will describe.

This book is also relevant to executives in midsized divisions of larger firms. While these managers can (in theory) draw upon the resources of their parent companies, in practice they often cannot. They're held to demanding financial targets with little assistance from corporate. In other words, they're really midsized companies—not Fortune 500 behemoths—with their top leaders reporting to other leaders higher up the corporate food chain.

The Invisible Middle

Despite how vital midsized companies are to our country's economic welfare, and despite how many of them there are, relatively little has been published over the years about what makes them tick. Even if you're a voracious reader of business books and publications, you probably haven't read much about the midsized business. That's not because thoughtful experts haven't weighed in from time to time; they have. But there are so very few of them. They're like sportswriters who cover pro bowling or lacrosse. Compared to the number of

pro baseball, basketball, and football writers, they're a van-
ishingly small cohort. There might be enough of them to orga-
nize a good book club.

Consequently, the midsized company has been grossly
underexamined. The light of the business experts, consultants, and professors has shined almost exclusively on the sexy
start-ups (especially those funded by venture capitalists and
located in that disruptive digital incubator, Silicon Valley) and
the equally compelling Fortune 500 goliaths.

"Despite its significance to the economy, the middle market
is an area about which we know much less than we know about
small firms and large firms," Anil Makhija, senior associate
dean at the Fisher College of Business, and academic director of
Ohio State University's National Center for the Middle Market,
told attendees at the research group's 2013 annual conference.
"Middle-market firms have been largely invisible."[2]

This blindness even affected the most recent presiden-
tial campaign. In the 2012 campaign, both President Barack
Obama and Republican nominee Mitt Romney focused on
small business. "Small businesses have always formed the
backbone of the American economy," the president said.[3]

Comparing the Middle Market to Small and Big Business

	Annual Revenue	Businesses	Employment
Small Business	<$10m	~6m	35%
Middle Market	$10m - <$1B	195,000	34%
Big Business	>$1B	~2,000	31%

FIGURE I-1:

Source: The Market That Moves America, *National Center for the Middle Market,
The Ohio State University, and GE Capital Corporation, October 2011.*

Well, in terms of sheer numbers, the president and ex-governor Romney were dead on. Almost six million small firms dot the U.S. landscape (companies with annual revenue of less than $10 million). That means small firms outnumber the 197,000 midsized firms by a factor of thirty.[4] But in terms of the mid-market's economic impact, both candidates were dead wrong. Not only do midsized businesses generate more revenue than small business, according to U.S. government data they account for nearly as many jobs (34 percent of the labor market versus 35 percent for small companies). And between 2007 and 2010, the middle market created 2.2 million jobs even as companies with revenue in excess of $1 billion cut their workforce.[6] Midsized firms have longevity that is nearly as good as big business, with 70 percent having survived twenty years or more, compared to only 16 percent for small business. Midsized companies are stable organizations that provide long-lasting jobs.

Company Longevity
Middle Market versus Small and Large

Sector	Median age of company	Longevity of company		
		■ <5 yrs	▨ 5-19 yrs	☐ 20+ yrs
Small Business	6 yrs	44%	71%	16%
Middle Market	31 yrs	4%	26%	70%
Large Business	35 yrs	4%	25%	71%

FIGURE I-2:

Source: The Market that Moves America, *National Center for the Middle Market, The Ohio State University and GE Capital Corporation, October 2011.*

I'd argue that the real backbone of the American economy is the midsized business.

Why Midsized Firms Are Different

So midsized companies are more important to the economy than most people realize. But, apart from the somewhat arbitrary revenue differentiator, what makes them special? What makes their problems—and the solutions to those problems—unique? In my work as a consultant to midsized businesses, and as a former CEO of a midsized business, I've found six factors in the DNA of midsized companies that set them apart from both larger and smaller companies and give rise to the distinctive challenges they face:

• **A low tolerance for risk.** Midsized firms have much more to lose than start-ups. They have many more employees that depend upon them, and their owners have a larger portion of their personal wealth at stake. Adding to their aversion to risk, midsized companies just aren't big enough to survive too many missteps. Their investors keep a vigil on profits and growth to fuel investment value, and typically pay no dividends. Start-ups, by contrast, are all about risk. If they fail, everybody goes out and gets a new job. Their investors know the risks and, in the case of venture capital and private equity, have diversified portfolios to manage them. Deep-pocketed Fortune 500 companies, of course, have the resources to experiment with new products and even new business models. They can assume great risks because they can write off multi-million-dollar failures. But in bootstrapping their small firms into midsized companies, many executives have survived hard times by being frugal. Such frugality makes them risk averse and often holds them back from getting to the next level. That would mean making risky investments in talent, infrastructure, research and development, and brand building.

• **High barriers to internal collaboration.** Midsized companies typically have more than a single office (or even more than a handful of offices), and their dispersed teams must communicate in order to conduct business. Yet they aren't so large as to be able to afford taking their managers away from their daily tasks to attend the off-sites or all-hands meetings that larger companies use to get everyone pumped up and aligned. Nor are they rich enough to pay for in-house organizational development teams or the other tools that big businesses use to keep top management in sync. Start-ups, on the other hand, typically have all their people in one place, focused on the same or closely related tasks at the same time, brewing their coffee in the same kitchen. Collaboration is easy when you're rinsing out your mugs in the same sink. Midsized firms are caught between critical mass and unencumbered nimbleness.

• **Few ways to develop talent.** Midsized firms (especially those growing quickly) typically don't have large HR functions to develop leaders, or the cash to invest in successor positions or training the way large corporations do. In slower-growing midsized firms, top managers can't (or won't) create adequate opportunities for advancement for younger talent, their future leaders. Midsized companies without multiple business units can't give aspiring leaders P&L responsibilities. In just about all midsized companies, it is rare to find executives who can spend time mentoring. Everyone is too busy doing his own job, making the business run.

• **Less investor patience for leaders learning on the job.** When a business is backed by venture capital or a private equity firm, there's a hard horizon for an expected return. Investors typically believe that the leaders of the businesses they put their money behind should have the skills they need to succeed. They're not interested in waiting for them to develop. If the leaders don't produce within the investors' timeline, they will be replaced. This can lead to a turnover rate at the top levels not experienced by smaller businesses (often run by their owners) or larger companies (in which leadership training is a core activity).

• **Less strategic thinking.** Big firms have chief strategy officers and teams dedicated to strategy, M&A, and corporate development. Start-ups have a central belief in one opportunity they race to embrace. Midsized firms, however, busy working to make the business they already have run profitably, often have to do their strategic thinking on the fly, with the part-time efforts of the CEO. Maybe, once or twice a year, they'll have an off-site at some nearby hotel equipped with a conference room. Bigger midsized firms ($300 million to $1 billion in revenue) might be able to afford a few senior executives in corporate development. In general, midsized firms don't have the time, inclination, or skills to consistently think strategically.

• **Less seasoned talent.** In midsized companies, a high percentage of owners, CEOs, and other leaders began at the bottom. They rose with the business, which means they may never have acquired or gotten the chance to polish the executive skills you see in Fortune 500 companies (and don't often need in smaller businesses and start-ups): disciplined planning, financial acumen, relationship building both inside and outside the business, talent development, mentoring, and leadership. Take any one of my law firm clients: great lawyers but no business training or experience. Another retail client started the business in college and grew it to over $300 million in revenues in twelve years, without ever holding more than a summer job as a teen.

Of course, the huge size range between $10 million and $1 billion in revenues means there is a great variety in the way

Three Segments in the Middle Market

Three distinct segments		
$10-50M	$50-100M	$100-1B
Operates more like smaller businesses, despite revenues	Consistent business practices; project strong growth	Resemble multinationals

$	$3.2T	$1.4T	$4.7T
Firms	156,000	21,000	18,000
Employees	16M	6M	18.7M

FIGURE I-3:

Source: The Market That Moves America, *National Center for the Middle Market, The Ohio State University, and GE Capital Corporation, October 2011.*

these firms conduct business. The National Center for the Middle Market divides the middle market into three segments. Naturally, those at the smaller end of the range have operations that are more like small businesses and, likewise, those at the top of the range act more like big businesses. In my own experience, most businesses squarely confront middlehood between $20 million and $500 million in revenues, depending on the rate of growth, the presence of external investors, the background of the CEO, and the competitiveness of the industry.

Like the soil and climate that determine the evolution of the flora and fauna in a specific region, these six limitations create the environment that affects the life and growth of the midsized firm. They also provide the ideal conditions for the emergence of the silent growth killers you will read about in this book.

The Seven Silent Growth Killers at a Glance

Not every midsized business wants to grow, but in my experience most need to show some growth to remain healthy, and many aspire to grow to the next level. Only some succeed. The others fall victim to one of the seven silent growth killers. These growth killers can slip in and set up shop in your boardrooms, executive suites, lunchrooms, sales floors, and factories before you even know they're there. Before you can begin to guard against them, you must learn to recognize all seven. They are:

1. *Letting Time Slip-Slide Away*

This growth killer is silent almost by definition because it has to do with that most ephemeral and subjective thing, time. When an organization loses its sense that time is a limited resource, deadlines on critical projects get pushed back with few if any consequences to the individuals and teams responsible. It's very easy to overlook time that slip-slides away, especially if a CEO allows it. Chapter 1 tells the story of how a laissez-faire attitude about time cost a $130 million retailer more than a million dollars as it tried to implement a critical new information system. It will then lay out four key ways that executives can create respect for time and deadlines. To illustrate these approaches, I will show how a new CEO at Goddard Systems Inc., franchisor of The Goddard School®, the fast-growing $530 million franchise system, created a culture—and a process for running productive meetings—that treated time with the type of respect it must receive if a midsized company is to grow.

2. *Strategy Tinkering at the Top*

Start-up companies must always be ready to tinker with their strategy. Because they are trying to tap previously unrecognized or unmet needs, they must tweak, adjust, and change course whenever they discover that those needs aren't exactly what they thought they were. Big companies simply don't tinker. They study, analyze, plan, and pilot. But for a midsized company, tinkering with the business's core strategy can be deadly. In chapter 2, I'll explain how Cellairis, in 2005 a $50 million–revenue wireless accessories company, took a 33 percent hit to its top line when it tinkered with its strategy, and how it recovered when it stopped. I'll also explain how Rodan + Fields, a $250 million skin-care products company, and the $500 million system-wide restaurant chain Jamba Juice instituted strategic and operational planning processes that avoided tinkering and kept them out of the business ditch.

3. *Reckless Attempts at Growth*

In describing this silent growth killer, I'll examine the problems of midsized firms that bungle their attempts to grow quickly, and I'll lay out three ways to take the "reckless attempt" out of growth. They are: gaining a deep understanding of your market, developing well-founded forecasts, and making evidence-based assessments of your ability to execute. I'll show in chapter 3 how preparing the ground in this manner helped BlueArc, a manufacturer of data storage gear, grow to $86 million in revenue during the Great Recession.

4. *Fumbling Strategic Acquisitions*

Companies often pursue growth by buying it. Sometimes that doesn't work out. When a corporate giant makes a bad acquisition, it usually has plenty of capital to absorb the loss. But when a midsized company makes a poor acquisition—even if the acquired firm is small—it can knock the company off course for years. Chapter 4 examines how poor acquisitions set back the growth of two midsized firms, a $130 million retailer and a $50 million food company. We'll explore why making a good acquisition is less about the deal and the closing, and more about what happens *afterward*: the integration process and execution of the acquisition plan. That's what largely determines whether an acquisition will make or lose money. I'll lay out four best practices for beating the odds against acquisition success (which are dreadful—two-to-one against, according to studies) through case studies on successful acquisitions at EORM (a $27 million environmental consulting firm), $360 million Pelican Products (a maker of cases for equipment), and United Site Services, a $120 million portable restroom provider (before they exited).

5. *Operational Meltdowns*

Small firms tend to notice problems in production, distribution, marketing, sales, or other critical processes early on. They have to. If they don't head off operational bugaboos, they'll wake up to find themselves out of business pretty quickly. Large companies typically have established written plans and performance metrics and people who are well paid to monitor them and to make sure there are no operational surprises. Midsized companies, however, usually lack both rigorous processes and dedicated operational troubleshooters. They are often surprised and overwhelmed by meltdowns in key processes, especially those that come from the always-difficult process of automating systems. In chapter 5, I'll discuss the four early signs that an operational meltdown is looming. I'll review the case of a company that rapidly grew to $50 million in revenue ahead of scalable infrastructure, leading to a rolling operational meltdown that compromised customer experience, was quite costly, and resulted in the dismissal of its logistics and IT heads. I'll also explore in depth what midsized companies—such as $53 million Dave's Killer Bread—have done to avoid such meltdowns.

6. *Liquidity Crashes*

Running out of money can happen to anyone. A dramatic economic downturn, the loss of a key customer, and other unexpected events can catch even the most experienced CEOs unprepared. In chapter 6, I'll tell the sad tale of a $70 million toy company that was pummeled by a liquidity crash in 2009 after a costly acquisition and a troubled warehouse system implementation led to a cash hemorrhage that ended up with its bank calling in its loans. But I'll also tell the story of a $30 million architecture firm that survived a 2008 crash in its market (retail store design) and lived to fight another day. The keys to emerging from a liquidity crisis, as this chapter explains, include building a strong balance sheet, monitoring cash flow, making smart and timely cost reductions (while avoiding harmful ones), and making sure you have the right investors in the business to begin with. You don't want impatient capital in times that require patience.

7. *Tolerating Dysfunctional Leaders*

When a business grows to midsize, it needs teams to handle projects and manage a larger workforce, and it needs leaders to manage the teams. Big companies can easily survive two or three weak links on a team of several dozen executives. But two or three weak links out of six or seven (the size of many midsized company management teams)? That's a recipe for disaster. Chapter 7 discusses the touchy subject of leaders who are not performing, how to spot them, and what to do about them. And to reduce the chance that you'll hire them in the first place, I'll lay out the ten critical elements of an effective recruiting strategy. I'll also show how companies such as a $30 million food manufacturer, $15 million CruiserCustomizing, and R. Torre & Company (a 125-person syrup manufacturer) took the bold step of removing talented, often-popular but no-longer-productive members of their top management team as a path to greater growth.

All seven growth killers are linked, and in the conclusion, you'll read a story where one killer brought on another, then another, until all seven had attacked. It's every CEO's nightmare. But because the killers are linked, there are steps all midsized businesses should take to reduce their vulnerability overall. In the conclusion, I lay out the concept of "leadership infrastructure." By this, I mean the sum total of all the management systems, processes, leadership teams, skill sets, and disciplines that enable companies to grow from small operations into midsized or large firms. It's very hard to build because one size doesn't fit all, and neglecting it is an open invitation to the silent growth killers. Yet it is the path to mightiness.

So What Makes Me So Smart?

Actually, I'm no smarter than the average bear, but for the past thirty years (unlike the average bear) I've operated in the executive suites of dozens of midsized companies. From 1984 to 2006, I was a founder and CEO of Bentley Publishing Group, and led the firm through four acquisitions that enabled it to become a leading player in the U.S. decorative art publishing industry. In fact, I published my first book about the lessons I learned on acquisitions (*The Feel of the Deal*)[7] the year after I left Bentley. Five years after I struck out on my own, the firm merged with another in 2011 to form the Bentley Global Arts Group.

After leaving Bentley in 2006, I launched a consulting business, CEO to CEO Inc., to help midsized companies get to the next level and to tackle many of the same issues I discuss in this book. Since 2007, I've worked with more than seventy-five midsized companies as a consultant to their CEOs and top management teams.

Since 1996, I've also been deeply involved in a community of top-level business leaders devoted to challenging common business wisdom and examining the strategic assumptions of business success. From 1996 to 2006, as CEO of Bentley, I was a member of the Alliance of Chief Executives, meeting monthly with a private group of CEOs. Once I left Bentley, I became a director of the Alliance and have since sat in on hundreds of Alliance CEO private group meetings. I lead an Alliance group of top executives from middle market companies (between $30 million and $800 million in revenues), facilitating deep discussions every month, listening to their challenges, and helping them see multiple perspectives so they can find solutions.

I've been writing about many of the lessons I've learned about the art and science of running midsized companies in two columns, one in *Forbes* magazine and the other on CFO. com. I've been a regular columnist at those publications since 2012. To write *Mighty Midsized Companies: How Leaders Overcome 7 Silent Growth Killers*, I interviewed more than a hundred CEOs at midsized companies, using their experiences and stories both to inform my thinking and to illustrate it.

This book is based on that research.

How to Use This Book

No matter what kind of midsized firm you are in, or hope to grow to become—whether it's a law firm or a dress manufacturer, a retail chain or a software company—this book should be used by your management team along with all the other good books in the marketplace on the strategies and pitfalls that attend growth.

CEOs, I hope, will find this book especially helpful as the

responsibility for dodging or dealing with the silent growth killers generally ends up at their door. But I didn't write this book solely for CEOs. Knowing the growth killers—and knowing what to do when they rear their ugly heads—will also enable heads of finance, sales, marketing, R&D, production, service, and other members of the leadership team to help their companies survive and thrive in these turbulent economic times.

Ultimately it will be the management team, working together and armed with an understanding of the seven silent growth killers, that will determine whether your business will fall victim to any one or all of them. I urge you to make the stories and lessons of this book the subject of management team meetings, especially if you believe one or more of the growth killers are already doing their dirty work in your organization.

If, as a team, you can learn to identify the early symptoms of a growth-killing infection, you'll be in a much better position to protect your company's health and ensure your midsized business's growth. And if you follow the steps I lay out to prevent the growth killers from taking root in the first place, as did many companies in the chapters that follow, your company will be able to stay productive and profitable all the days of its life. It will be mighty.

That's what you want; that's what I want for you.

1

Letting Time Slip-Slide Away

When companies grow from small firms into midsized ones, they're a lot like settlers arriving in a strange new land. There's a lot to do and not a lot of time to do it in. When the Pilgrims first dropped anchor in November 1620 and rowed ashore, they needed more than shelter. They needed to find water and food. And it was a lot colder than they expected, so they had to make new, warmer clothing. And it behooved them to establish friendly relations with the people they found living there who (reasonably) weren't all that happy about these outlandish newcomers moving into their neighborhood.

Of course, the Pilgrims couldn't accomplish everything they needed to get done in a day or a month or even a year. It took a long time, and a lot of the original *Mayflower* passengers (over 50 percent) didn't make it. The same is true of growing midsized businesses.

The world is littered with the remnants of firms that tried to do too much and spent too big on growing up. They invested in new buildings. They implemented new computer systems. And then, unlike the Massachusetts Bay Colony, they stopped growing and the overhead on all that new stuff became hard to manage.

And often they failed to get everything they needed. Perhaps they got shelter (buildings), but clean water was hard to come by. Building a dependable water supply seemed to take forever. Why? Perhaps it's because the company never built a water supply system before so what did they know about it?

Bigger firms have more resources than midsized businesses; they rarely outgrow their infrastructure all at once. Small companies can be scrappy and make do. They can assign someone to rush out and carry back a bucket of water (after all, they don't need all that much). But midsized firms, which need to do many things and undertake many large projects at the same time, must learn to prioritize and plan. And as they do, they need to understand that time—just like the Pilgrims—is not on their side. Time. This is the first silent killer of midsized company growth.

Work + Time = More Than You Think

How can time (or rather, a lack of appreciation for it) be a killer?

Let me show you.

In 2012 the top management of a $130 million retailer realized that after years of rapid growth the firm had outgrown the enterprise resource planning (ERP) software it installed when it was a $30 million business. The retailer wanted to expand internationally, but the old ERP wasn't up to the task. Not only that, but with hundreds of retail locations, the company had no unified point-of-sale (POS) system. That should have been installed at least five years earlier and the CEO, a first-time entrepreneur, had made it a priority. But he had other priorities, like opening a retail website to drive revenue, and designing an innovative new product that could differentiate the company, and developing an app to leverage mobile shopping, and, and...

The good news was that the company was healthy and debt-free. The bad news was that it had no CFO, and the engineering VP who ran the company's four-person IT team had never done an ERP upgrade. But a few executives who had been with the retailer from the start teamed up with a software vendor and picked the new ERP system.

The CEO approved it and the company purchased its new system in June 2012 through a value-added reseller (VAR) that would find a host for the software in the cloud and coach the company through the software vendor's installation. The retailer paid the vendor $152,000 for the software, entered into a $1.1 million contract with the VAR for its training and hosting services, and retained the software vendor to install the system and to help guide the project.

The engineering VP went right to work customizing the new ERP and preparing to connect it to the firm's other systems. But the VP was a busy guy and his other priorities—getting the POS system right, building the retail website, developing the mobile app, keeping the old ERP running—kept getting in the way. Meanwhile, the VAR wasn't doing much training (it had assigned fairly low-level people to the project and they were waiting for instructions from the company's leadership) and the software vendor wasn't making much progress on the installation as it was waiting for the VP to complete his customizations.

The cutover date was set for October 2012. But as the leaves began to fall, everyone (the CEO, the engineering VP, the controller) agreed (in an ad hoc way) that the target date was too optimistic. They didn't set a new date, and they didn't assign anyone to report regularly on the project's status.

The company's business leaders weren't all that focused. The CEO was concerned with customer issues, new product development, and more. The controller was agonizing over the accounting. The company's leadership was overwhelmed. Meanwhile, the project progressed (if you want to call it that) in fits and starts.

Actually, even calling it a project would be an overstatement.

While IT had a list of customizations it was supposed to make to the system, there was no dedicated in-house project manager. Necessary financial reports and system changes were put on hold. After all, it didn't make sense to do them before the new ERP system was up and running, as they would only have to be redone. But there was no new ERP system. Meanwhile, the old one was becoming ever less useful as the company tried to grow into new overseas markets.

In May 2013 the retailer brought me in to introduce more rigorous business planning to the organization. Of course, the new ERP system—actually, the absence of the new ERP— came up in our initial discussions. Everyone thought it was someone else's responsibility. They decided that, as no one knew the new ERP software (and no one in the company had ever led an ERP implementation), they should hire someone who did. So they did—almost a year after the project started.

Midsized companies like this retailer regularly commit to big, complex projects without in-house expertise. Often, they need such expertise only for a few months, so they ask, "Why hire it?" After all, how often does a company install a new ERP? Worse still, many midsized companies have rookie executives on board (who joined when the firm was small) who have never managed large projects, nor learned how to assess the competencies of self-proclaimed experts inside or outside the firm.

Ultimately, the company found an excellent IT contractor who knew the software and had trained teams in the past. They hired him for a six-month stint. Good. He set up a training room. The engineering VP committed to an October 2013 cutover date. The VAR was dismissed and the contract terminated, but the cloud hosting firm was still being paid $20,000 per month. For $6,000 a week, the new contractor was doing ten times what the VAR had done for a tenth of the cost.

But the company was not yet out of the woods. So much

time had elapsed since it had purchased the software that a new version had been released and the retailer had to upgrade (and adjust its customizations) even before it began using it.

The CEO also realized that it was time to hire a CFO. The new CFO started on July 15, 2013. Within six weeks, it became clear to him that an October cutover would be unwise. The engineering VP had not fully understood some significant business needs the system had to address, and the business leaders still needed to do a lot of work to define system requirements. It was all too much to accomplish in three months. And doing the conversion just before the retailer's peak season was simply a terrible idea.

About then the CEO, who was frustrated by how slow and undependable the company's headquarters' network was, asked the engineering VP to hire a consultant to assess the problem. The consultant's verdict? The company's IT hardware infrastructure wouldn't be able to handle the new ERP system. It would have to rewire and build a server room to host the software. That would cost $180,000.

With the new CFO's guidance, a new cutover date was set for March 2014. He wrote a detailed plan and took responsibility for seeing it through. The company could now see light at the end of the tunnel, and it was fairly confident that when March arrived, so would the cutover.

Even before that hoped-for cutover, the ERP rollout had cost the company $152,000 for the software; $436,000 for the VAR; $360,000 in hosting fees for eighteen months (in which nothing was hosted); $180,000 for the new infrastructure; $190,000 for the contractor's services; and $80,000 for the IT consulting firm that advised it on the software. That adds up to nearly $1.4 million, not including the salaries of several in-house programmers who worked on the customizations for the better part of a year, or the time spent managing the changes, configuring the system, testing it, and running parallel systems while the new system was being worked on. It also doesn't take into account the eighteen months of lost opportunities that the new system was purchased to provide, and the extra people the company had to employ and pay over that time.

Of course, many ERP installations cost much more and take even longer. But this case is instructive as it highlights a particular problem that affects midsized businesses far more than it does both larger and smaller enterprises: a lack of respect for time.

Our retailer went shopping for all the things it needed and considered them all equally important. Heading out to explore the new world of overseas markets, the company had no realistic idea how much time any of the steps would take.

It's not surprising that it met none of its target dates.

Without understanding the real costs and benefits of any initiative, it's impossible to prioritize. Without prioritizing, it's impossible to dedicate resources appropriately. Without disciplined management of those resources, nothing gets done—at least, not very well, and certainly not on time or on budget.

Time and money. You've heard of them. As a businessperson, I know you respect money. But do you give equal respect to time? Is a minute wasted as disconcerting to you as a dollar discarded?

It should be.

Time: Your Most Important Resource

The atmosphere at small companies is always drenched in urgency. While their projects tend to be small, the stakes are always high. With limited resources, a small firm must see a quick return on every investment. Small businesses live close to the edge.

But as small businesses grow, they can lose that sense of urgency. Bigger projects get handled by teams, not individuals, and responsibility, if it is assigned at all, is distributed.

Deadlines slide. Things don't get done and no one is called to task. The organization loses its time sense, the concept that its passage must produce results.

Larger businesses can afford the luxury of dedicated project teams. However, most leaders at midsized businesses have other responsibilities even as they are tasked with driving or supporting special projects.

In business, every hour is precious. Time is a resource to be spent wisely. When time is no longer considered a gift whose value decreases with every tick of the clock, when deadlines are missed and meetings drag on without decisions being made, your competition can slip through those lost moments and steal your market and customers.

Midsized firms must accomplish their projects on time, or their growth will stall. As midsized businesses grow, either by entering new markets, launching new products, or acquiring other companies, they must tackle increasingly complex projects. They will need to implement new controls to comply with regulations in new jurisdictions or upgrade information systems to integrate acquired businesses (see chapter 4, "Fumbled Strategic Acquisitions"). Bigger projects demand careful planning and diligent project management. These projects will absorb more of a company's finite resources, and at midsized companies there frequently are multiple projects proceeding at the same time.

Many projects directly affect the customer experience. The CEO must realize if the company does not take care of the customer through great execution, some other company will. After all, time is money, and money is the customer. Master time, and you'll master the customer.

Even firms that do a reasonable job of planning may crash and burn when they have to shift resources from one project to another due to a crisis or a shortfall in another area. Sometimes these businesses just don't have adequate project management skills and haven't learned how to stay on track during long projects.

Eventually, the frustrated CEO will shout, "Why can't we get things done around here anymore?"

Many CEOs then deliver the famous tough talk. They jump up and down, but too often they themselves don't know how to fix the underlying problems: lack of planning knowledge and decision-making discipline; lack of project management skills; an unwillingness to hold people accountable or to set clear priorities and stick by them. CEOs can bring project managers into their companies. But while these new hires will bring needed skills, they won't be able to change the culture of the company by themselves. All too often, they end up doing little more than reporting on how late the projects are.

I've developed an online assessment to determine if (and how severely) time is slipping away and the extent to which this silent growth killer is affecting your company. You'll find it at www.ceotoceo.biz/mightytools.html.

The ultimate solution for midsized company CEOs who see their most important projects withering on the vine is to instill a new respect for time throughout the business. And that begins with enforcing the discipline of planning.

Take Back the Clock

To make the most of the time within which a company has to accomplish a given project, the leader must draw a line in the sand (dramatizing the deadline and the importance of the project), with weekly, or even daily, tasks planned in advance, and with someone given the responsibility for meeting these deadlines. Assigning clear responsibilities means facing the fact that (to paraphrase the Rolling Stones) we can't always get what we want; but if we try, we can get what we need.

Once we assign responsibility for a project, we may come to realize that the person tasked with the project's completion may not have what it takes. That's good to know, the earlier the better. Midsized firms don't have a lot of management depth. We may also get pushback that can illuminate problems with the project's concept. That's also good. Holding someone accountable for something that's impossible is folly.

Assigning responsibility must be combined with regular oversight to insure the timely completion of each step in the project and a regular cadence of communication between the team and all affected parties. This is especially important in midsized firms where leaders may be forced to stretch the competencies of the leadership team. There should be no surprises, and nothing should be hidden.

A keen sense of time can be created in four ways:

1. *Time boxing.* Picking a single point on the calendar and agreeing that that is the deadline increases the pressure on everyone to perform. When a company decides to exhibit at a trade show, for example, time boxing is automatic. The show will go on. You either finish the project (in this case, your exhibition) on time, or the show will open without you and you'll lose your deposit. The time box, whether internally or externally imposed, sharpens the organization's appreciation of time.

2. *Expectations.* If your organization has any project management competence or discipline at all, expecting timely results will create pressure, which will force you to plan. The trade show is a good case in point. Knowing that you can't postpone or miss it, you *have* to have a plan to deliver. That means creating schedules of tasks to be completed and the deadlines that go with them.

3. *Prioritization.* Planning forces us to prioritize the specific steps we must take. It also demands that we anticipate events that might affect those steps. Consequently, we budget for extra time, knowing that problems inevitably crop up. This drives us to assess our vulnerabilities and create backup plans for everything. It also forces us to assess our resources (primarily money and time). We may have to take other items off our plate in the process of prioritizing.

Containing and Maintaining
Pressure Produces Timely Results

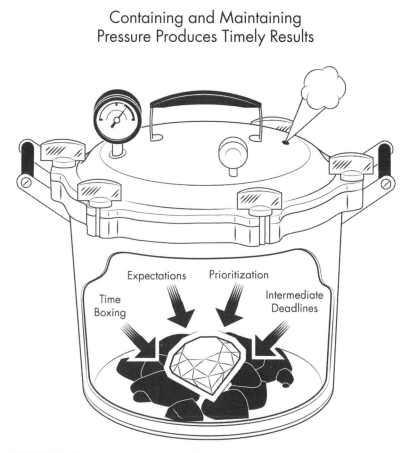

FIGURE 1-1: Just as coal turns to diamonds when under enough pressure, organizations that create and contain the right amount of pressure will generate timely as well as higher quality results.

4. *Intermediate deadlines.* Approaching deadlines give us a heightened sense of time passing and keep us focused on our priorities. Given that we've broken the project down into discrete steps, a deadline is *always* approaching, and that creates urgency and focus and prevents time from being frittered away.

How Goddard Systems Changed Its Sense of Time

Despite many successes and the best of intentions, Goddard Systems Inc., a Pennsylvania-based national franchisor of The Goddard School® preschool system, found itself in 2007 missing deadline after deadline as it tried to rewrite its franchisee training manual.

A training manual is a fundamental tool franchisors use to capture best practices and disseminate them efficiently. Over seventeen years, Goddard had grown to two hundred geographically dispersed locations nationwide and its old manual was out of date. It called for too much one-on-one training for new franchisees and employees. If Goddard wanted to scale for tomorrow, a new manual was necessary.

But the new manual was not necessary to *today's* operations, and other projects always seemed to come first. The company's current franchisees had learned The Goddard School® approach well. Consequently, despite the fact that everyone knew a new manual would be useful and needed eventually, it wasn't getting done. It was and was not a priority. When a new leader (and now CEO), Joe Schumacher, joined the senior management team in 2007, he recognized the fundamental problem: at Goddard Systems Inc., time was not appreciated as a valuable resource.

Schumacher required his management team to develop strong business cases for each project. That helped everyone differentiate high-priority initiatives from low-priority ones. And it forced senior managers to identify precisely the resources their projects required. Schumacher also made rewriting the training manual a *real* priority because he knew that rapid expansion was just around the corner, and when that happened, if Goddard didn't have the new manual, training (and performance) would suffer. Responsibility for getting it done was assigned. And it got done.

Today, the firm has grown to more than four hundred locations, and the management team is continually trained on project management techniques. Goddard now regards project management as a fundamental executive skill. Its 2012 launch of Goddard Connect—a web portal that facilitates communication and collaboration among franchisees—was delivered on time and on budget. That was a dramatic change from what Schumacher found in 2007.

To create a corporate culture that treats time as a valuable commodity in short supply, the CEO must believe it's true. All the process and project management in the world will be for naught if the CEO doesn't walk the talk. And that doesn't mean simply setting deadlines and demanding that they be met. Unless the CEO intimately understands what meeting the deadline entails in time and resources, those deadlines inevitably will be unrealistic and they will *not* be met. Soon, making excuses for not meeting deadlines will become the company norm. The shift from a casual attitude toward time to an insistence for on-time completion must include a diligent process to develop realistic deadlines. That attitude must flow from the top.

Many companies that let time and deadlines slip away need an outsider such as Schumacher, acting at an executive level, to change the environment. That person might be a new CFO, another member of the C-suite, a consultant or interim executive, or even a new chair of the board. This is especially true for executive teams that have worked together for a long time.

The new leader must be a strong advocate for the change and start making it stick as soon as he or she arrives. The new leader, along with the rest of the top team, must model the new behavior in his or her actions, and instill the concept of planning. Planning is the way midsized companies optimize their use of time.

Prioritization: Harnessing Time

Every businessperson knows there's a difference between must-haves and like-to-haves. But sometimes it's not so easy to tell one from the other. In fact, the closer you are to your business, the harder it becomes. This can make prioritization a challenge, one that often requires an outsider to make the hard call and say one initiative is important, another less so.

One fast-growing consumer products company had for several years bitten off too much, and consequently had not completed major projects that would help HR, IT, and systems-related quality assurance—all critical support functions. As it became clear to the CEO that top team competency and leadership infrastructure were issues, loyalty to struggling team members and continued external focus got in the way of making the critical adjustments. Productivity and innovation slowed as employees struggled with manual processes and past-their-prime suppliers and technologies. Customers were becoming unhappy with service and support. As these unfinished projects absorbed needed resources, the company's business was suffering and its future growth imperiled.

I was the outsider this time. The executive team and I looked at the whole company, its forecasted revenues, and free cash flow. We had to understand its financial realities for the coming year to understand the resources we would have for the projects on the table.

Then we sketched out a company-level plan. This was

a sketch, not a final draft. I had to help the executive team understand its most important top-level goals and with those goals in mind, devise a strategy for going forward. The top team gathered and prioritized projects, eliminating some and identifying others as must-haves. Everyone fought hard for what she believed were the most important projects. This took several days and it wasn't fun. Some people were disappointed that their pet projects died. Some got emotional. The team cared deeply about the company and had strong opinions about the right path forward.

These conflicts are not a bad thing; in fact, they are necessary to make good decisions. It never works to consider projects one at a time because that means there is no competition for resources. But no company's resources—especially a midsized company's—are unlimited. If projects are not placed in competition with each other, they can't be fit like pieces in a puzzle into the big picture of a company's resources and longer-term strategy.

By the end of the planning sessions, we were close to balancing the business's resources with its critical projects. Some projects were slimmed down, some were cut, and some were expanded. Some people felt they had not persuaded others to their views; some felt like winners. But the biggest winner was the company, which was now on the path toward accomplishing the *right* projects that would support its growth goals. And by narrowing the field, the attitude toward accomplishing projects on time moved from "I wish we could" to "I know we can."

If your company is letting time (and therefore money and opportunity) slip through its fingers, and if its failure to complete projects on time and on budget is killing its growth potential, there are three steps you can take to meet the enemy and vanquish it.

1. *Prioritize.* Here's the awful truth that every ambitious, creative, hard-charging CEO must come to grips with: even if you're the boss, there are limits to what you can accomplish.

Some CEOs want every project to be a top priority. Others struggle to say no when their direct reports push them to green-light their pet projects. Ultimately, if a company tries to do too much with too few resources and too little time, projects—if they're completed at all—will be late. They probably also will be done poorly, no matter how diligent the project management. CEOs must make hard choices about which projects are most important to the business. It's those projects that should get the CEO's full attention; it's those projects that should be funded as richly as possible.

A project is only as good as the resources that support it. Good planning should reserve resources and compare the likely availability of resources (based on forecasts of business performance and staffing projections) with the investment required for each project to succeed. The worst thing a mid-sized business can do is to start five projects that are barely affordable and then have to cancel (or fail to complete) the three most important ones because the resources just aren't there. Invest heavily in the most important projects. And to increase the likelihood of on-time completion, leave some slack in the budget. That will allow you to absorb surprises and still finish on plan.

2. *Plan.* For those projects not crossed off the list when you prioritize, the functional teams responsible for their completion must write detailed plans containing all the steps to complete the project, including all the resources that will be needed and all the results expected. Each project should have a one- to two-page summary written to insure that everyone understands the project's resources, stages, and goals. Each task should have

start and end dates, and a champion should be assigned to be accountable. Making the project as transparent as possible, especially to the board, adds pressure on the executive team to ensure that the schedule is adhered to and the job gets done. I've developed a ten-point planning tool that helps anyone to think through a project and write down the essentials. It's available online at www.ceotoceo.biz/mightytools.html

3. *Manage.* I used to think that a manager's job was to get things done. (Actually, I still do.) But many people who hold the titles of managing director, vice president, or higher seem to lack experience in basic project management. Understanding how to do it doesn't require a project management program or a certificate in project management. Managing a project is often as simple as breaking up a big task into a series of small steps, with start and finish dates and a person in charge of each step, and then jumping on each step at the predetermined time and seeing it through.

Many people will say, "But we already do all that at our company." If you do, then please go and retrieve the document that captures the details for each project. I'm betting that many of you won't find it. I've said this before and I'll say it again: *In business, nothing is real if it is not written down.*

Here are three review and visibility techniques that connect any project to the passage of time:

- A *calendar*, actively managed by someone on the team. The calendar should report on the project's progress at least once a week. This makes the project visible to others in the organization. When we know someone is charting our progress, we all pay extra attention.
- A *monthly review*, presented publicly (in brief) to the project leader's peers, noting whether the project is on

schedule. If it's not, the review should contain the corrective actions that need to be taken. This cadence of communication (and its visibility) is critical to completing the project on time.

- *A quarterly review,* updating the board on the project's progress. This is a less frequent cadence but even more powerful because of the nature of its audience, and because it acknowledges the passage of time in a more holistic manner.

Meetings: Time's a-Wasting

I know. You all know about project management. You either learned it in business school or through hands-on experience. And, at some level, you all understand the value of time and the importance of not wasting it. But you also know that many of your cherished projects are late, and many others…well, you don't know what the heck happened to them.

Why is this happening? What's getting in the way of good project execution? Could it be your meetings?

Once a business grows past a certain size, it takes teams to accomplish tasks. For teams to work effectively, they have to meet. And although meetings are frequently disparaged ("A meeting is an event in which the minutes are kept but the hours are lost"), they are essential to business. They are especially essential to the execution of projects. And even companies that prioritize, plan, and manage diligently can have bad meetings that sabotage projects by wasting the participants' time.

*The problem doesn't lie in the act of meeting; it lies in the process of **running** meetings.*

If they are positive in tone, poorly run meetings will feel like brainstorming sessions (often repetitive). If the tone is neutral, they'll seem like updates, and if the energy is negative, they'll sound like complaint sessions. While there are certainly times for all these types of meetings, the time *isn't* when the purpose of the meeting is to plan or execute an important initiative.

Poorly run meetings are most often the product of a lack of preparation by all parties involved. Critical, complex issues require study, research, and testing before a final decision is made. Too often, people come together not having done their homework and waste time in conjecture and opinion. Deep down, they know that making a decision without adequate information would be risky, as indeed it would, so no decision is made and another meeting is scheduled for sometime down the road. And the next meeting assuredly will be a repeat of the last if the participants are not prepared.

Making the most of meetings requires discipline: the discipline to define a clear purpose for the meeting, to stick to that purpose, and to insist that the only people who participate have a good reason for being there. Wanting to be in on the action is not a good reason. The only good reason for someone to be invited to a meeting is because they have something to contribute.

In companies that respect time, people are allergic to meetings that meander and don't end with actions to be taken. They want the meetings they attend to be at least as fruitful as the time they spend working at their desks. The trick is to have the right number of meetings, with the right participants, with every meeting well run. Here are some of the things you need to have to make your meeting productive. Consider them over-the-counter medicine for the meeting-allergic.

Leadership

Nothing runs well in an organization without a single point of control. It's the same with a meeting. A debate, lest it spiral out of control and end up wasting everyone's time, requires a referee who can call a halt. A well-facilitated meeting has a person who controls the debate, makes sure the group comes to a decision, and documents that decision.

Facilitating a meeting takes strength. It may require stopping some people from talking while encouraging others. It may require driving a decision over the objections of a participant. More than anything, facilitation means following a process within the meeting. The role of facilitator should be assigned, and that person should be empowered by the most senior member in the meeting.

There are many times when good facilitation can result in a consensus-based decision, but that is not always the case. Sometimes, when there is an impasse, it takes the leader of the business unit to step in and impose a decision on the team. In the absence of such a leader, or if the leader cannot or will not make the call, the debate may never end. There is no substitute for leaders with the courage to make well-informed judgment calls.

Debate

Debate is not bad. On the contrary, people who care about the organization need to be able to express themselves. Sometimes, that expression takes the form of a vigorous argument, and that can make some people uncomfortable. That's healthy and normal as long as everything is kept professional, impersonal (in the best sense), and focused on the problem at hand. The bigger the decision, the more time must be spent airing all the arguments and letting team members try to persuade one another. It is in the give-and-take of discussion and dispute that team members connect and discover new ideas and approaches. Leaders who stifle debate and send the team back to their corners will find that the debate reemerges, perhaps in another form, to consume another meeting because it was never fully resolved in the first place.

Some people will fall silent in a debate even though they disagree. They will air their opinions later, often in less productive venues, trying to derail the decision or otherwise manipulate the process. This is toxic to the business, and the leader should not allow it. If the leader sees someone who seems to disagree with the trend of the discussion or the decision at which the team has arrived but is holding back, the leader should do everything possible to draw the person out so that all opinions are aired in front of everyone. This requires the sensitivity to identify the person who is silently disgruntled and the strength to confront him.

Documentation

As I've said, *in business, nothing is real if it has not been written down.* Not documenting what is said at a meeting will ensure that whatever has been decided will be revisited at another meeting, with the same debate repeating itself. It will also provide an opportunity for the meeting's sore losers, those whose ideas have not prevailed in open debate, to reopen the discussion and cause... another meeting.

When capturing the meeting in writing, be sure to include the decision itself, why it was made, and who is responsible for executing the decision by what deadline. Note the assumptions that were used to guide the decision so that if there's a change in the business environment that requires a change in course, the discussion doesn't have to cover old ground. It is also important to list the alternatives that were discussed and why they were not chosen. (Failing to capture discarded ideas opens a window through which they can be reintroduced, wasting everyone's time.)

It is useful to record what the decision's results are expected to be. Checking back on whether these results were achieved is a way to determine whether the decision and the assumptions used to arrive at it were valid.

Finally, list the trigger points at which the decision should be reevaluated. For example, "If the launch produces less than $400,000 in revenue in the second month, we'll reconvene to reassess." This will help the business avoid the trap of sticking with a bad decision and wasting time by arguing when and how to reconsider it.

The amount of documentation a business requires for its meetings will vary depending on the team's behavior. If meetings that produce debates without decisions are a chronic problem, you'll need a lot of documentation. But as your meetings improve, as debate becomes more productive and less contentious, you may need heavy documentation only for the most critical meetings and decisions.

Now's the Time

Pushing new projects toward completion on time and within budget is hard work. It stretches a company's resources and forces people to make hard choices. It places huge burdens on a company's leaders. Frankly, it's easier to let things slide. Who needs the pressure? Who likes working with a clock ticking loudly in your ear? But no business can afford to stand still. No business can afford to let time and deadlines slip. Failing to initiate necessary and forward-looking projects is almost as guaranteed a growth killer as failing to complete them in a timely manner once they've begun.

You can get awfully thirsty if you don't get around to finishing your settlement's water system.

To make time work for the business, not against it, CEOs need to be clear about the consequences of not completing projects in general, and each specific project in particular. If, as CEO, you prioritize, plan, and execute those plans well in pursuit of an agreed-upon company goal, your businesses will accomplish more in a shorter time frame and you'll grow to new levels.

And then time will be on your side.

2
Strategy Tinkering at the Top

In early 2000, Taki Skouras, Joseph Brown, and Jaime Brown started Cellairis to sell wireless phone accessories, mostly cell phone cases. With very little start-up cash, they looked for inexpensive retail sites. They found them in those carts that sit in the middle of shopping malls.

By 2005, Cellairis had 150 stores (some operating as franchises) in malls, and approximately $50 million in system-wide annual revenue.

From nothing to $50 million in five years is phenomenal growth, and in 2006 the founders hired an experienced president to manage it.

The new president immediately began tinkering with Cellairis's strategy. He found a wireless provider, AMP'd Mobile, a reseller for the major carriers. AMP'd wanted to partner with Cellairis to grow its market share. Skouras, the CEO, who was excited by the possibility of offering customers an extra something, approved of the venture. Without testing the concept, Cellairis opened AMP'd stores in the malls.

Nine months later, AMP'd, having underpriced its services and lavishly extended credit to customers to gain market share, couldn't pay Cellairis or its carriers. AMP'd filed for bankruptcy. It cost Cellairis millions to unwind the program; Cellairis's president was dismissed, and by 2007 its sales had dropped 33 percent.

Cellairis had taken a market strategy that was working and then tinkered with it. Strategy tinkering is a casual, almost cavalier adjustment to a company's core strategy.

Strategy tinkering at the top. This is the second silent killer of midsized company growth.

The Middle: The Worst Place to Tinker

There are lots of reasons companies begin to tinker with their strategy. Some CEOs become nervous about poor or less-than-forecasted results. Sometimes, as was the case with Cellairis, tinkering comes from exuberance about a promising opportunity that suddenly surfaces.

Other companies never adequately articulate their core strategy. And that means their top team keeps multiple, often conflicting strategies alive that beg for tinkering. But strategy tinkering always leaves a firm vulnerable.

Such tinkering usually doesn't affect start-ups. Not yet having a core business that absorbs their energies, they can move quickly on hunches, chasing after new market opportunities. Changing strategies and pivoting quickly and repeatedly is the norm for start-ups. Without that flexibility, even more of them would die. Look how fast a little start-up called Facebook—which began as a dating service for Harvard kids—tinkered until it sewed up online social networking as far-bigger competitors (Microsoft, Yahoo, and Google, to name just a few) watched enviously.

Small but long-established businesses are on the other end of the spectrum, especially those that aren't venture-funded. They typically stick to what they know; they're risk averse and wary of spending to chase new opportunities. (Not that they have the access to capital needed to fund the chase in the first place.) To survive, small businesses need to stick to their knitting. They need to be fixated on their vision, and on execution.

Large companies, of course, want and need to innovate. They have to find new opportunities for growth; their shareholders demand it. But because of their size, they naturally run pilots and market tests off to the side where they won't interfere with their core businesses. They can launch new brands and sometimes even new companies without materially affecting their core or depleting their financial resources (as a smaller business would). These pilots and launches don't overtax their leadership teams, as they have multiple levels of leadership.

But midsized companies suffer when they are diverted from their core business. The leadership teams driving execution are not large enough that they can go off to experiment without adversely affecting operations. And midsized businesses tend not to have the resources (or discipline) to test a new strategy in a pilot, or off to the side. Quite often, a CEO who feels his company has become too dependent on a single customer, or is stuck in a shrinking or too-crowded market, will decide to tinker with the company's strategy. He will grab a half dozen of his most talented executives and steal their hours and energies to work out some new ideas. Since it's the CEO asking, the executives can't say they're too busy. They drop or give less time to their work in order to brainstorm and tinker along with the CEO.

Think of your core business like a freeway, with never-ending execution happening (hopefully) at high speed. Imagine what would happen if somebody started driving an untested experimental jalopy that couldn't keep up—one that in fact kept breaking down. Imagine the nasty traffic jam and hundreds of frustrated drivers. Progress would come to a screeching halt.

The Freeway Is No Place for Tinkerers to Experiment

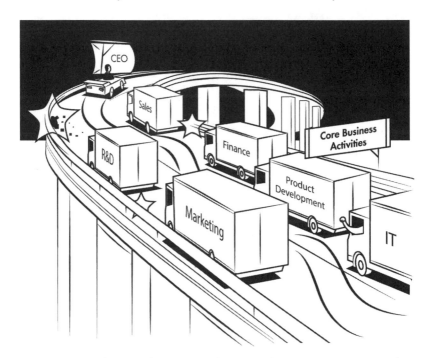

FIGURE 2-1: When tinkering at the top slows down or impedes progress for the company's core business, tempers flare and everyone suffers. Where's the competition in this illustration? Way down the road.

The Publisher with Too Many Ideas

An online book publisher had a solid, steady business that had been producing cash for a number of years. The CEO wanted the firm to grow, and began writing up his plan, breaking it down for each of his leaders. So far so good. But he enjoyed the planning work so much that he couldn't stop. Within a month, he announced that he had a new, better idea to scale the business, and rearranged his management team's priorities to pursue it. All the previous plans had to be revised.

Within a few weeks, however, the new strategy was looking less attractive, and the CEO noticed that the core business was not getting the attention it needed and deserved. Upset, he demanded that his team refocus on quality. Yet within a month, the tinkering passion overcame him and he came up with another new, irresistible idea. Again, he directed his team to pursue it, with similarly poor results. He was steering his entire company from guardrail to guardrail, and his firm's forward progress was imperiled.

A year later, most of his top team was gone. Some were fired; some fled. Quality leaders don't want to stay in a place where they are set up to fail. The publisher's revenues declined, and the spirit of the enterprise had been broken. Why invest energy in any one strategy if you know it will soon be replaced by a new idea du jour?

Tinkerers are impulse driven, and often fail to do their homework. One multi-store toy retailer decided to expand vertically, effectively competing with the importer that supplied it. The importer's CEO got really mad and decided that two could play that game. So he bought a retailer for $4 million. His impulse was wrong, and the retailer he bought was the wrong one. Not only was the retailer he bought losing money, it didn't know why, and it had no controller or CFO.

So not only had the CEO not acquired the capability to compete with his old customer (a strategic failure), he was now the not-so-proud owner of a failing retailer that he had to fix (an operational challenge).

But, of course, how could the CEO have predicted that? After all, he was just tinkering. You'll read more about the gory details of this importer's encounters with all seven silent growth killers in this book's concluding chapter.

The Cure for Tinkering: Planning

We've seen some examples of what can come from tinkering, from impulsively changing core business strategies without testing, without thinking it through. This is not to say that a company's strategy should never change. That would be as bad as tinkering. But if a strategy needs to change, it has to change in a thoughtful way, and that involves planning.

Planning comes in two flavors: strategic and operational. You should do both. Planning will not only help you change your strategy when you need to, it will protect your business from the urge to tinker. But you should never mix the two. Here's why:

Strategic Planning

Strategic planning is about figuring out the right thing to do. That could be sticking with what the business is already doing, or moving on to something new. Strategic planning addresses the problem of what you *should* be doing, not how well you're doing it. Business conditions change. What you're doing right today may not be right tomorrow.

Strategic planning requires a deep examination of a company's business model. It attempts to forecast the company's position in the marketplace three to five years out (or longer for big or capital-intensive firms). It identifies the company's strengths, weaknesses, opportunities, and the threats (or SWOT for short) it faces today, and strives to envision the SWOT of the future, as well as how the company must adapt. For example, strategic planning famously led IBM, a computer company, to become a consulting and technology firm. IBM asked itself where it wanted to be in five years, and saw that just making computers wasn't it.

A solid strategic planning process looks at a company's

competitive positioning, shifts in customer demand and preferences, adjacent industries, industry maturation, and more. Consulting firms like Bain and McKinsey love to lead strategic planning exercises. A diligent effort on a strategic plan can take hundreds of hours of top management's time—time taken away from running the business. The investment is significant—seven-figure sums are not unusual—and that's usually too much for midsized firms. They must do a slimmed-down version of strategic planning.

Operational Planning

Operational planning, on the other hand, is about doing things right. Every even moderately successful midsized company does something right, and it must continue to do whatever that is well to sustain the business. If a company gets sloppy about running its core business, it will shrink.

Operational planning focuses on the year ahead. It identifies and prioritizes projects for each person on the leadership team, with goals and deadlines captured in a document. It includes monthly objectives and key performance indicators (KPIs) for each leader. Good operational planning requires that all the functions confer so the pieces of the plan are synchronized, and the proper support functions (finance, IT, HR) are calibrated to help.

In operational planning mode, the business focuses on execution, setting aside all the possible opportunities and threats that surround it. The job is to make the most of the strategy it has already selected.

Strategic planning requires zero-based thinking. By that I mean it sets aside any presumptions about its current strategy and looks at all the options and realities that present themselves without regard to investments already made. This kind of thinking is threatening, unnerving, and often distracting to most people in a business, especially employees and middle managers.

That's why it's a good practice to do strategic planning and operational planning separately. Blending them distracts the team from execution, and results in a lack of depth in both. Don't fall prey to the temptation to "be efficient" and do them together: it is a trap to avoid.

Many firms kick off a full strategic planning process every three to five years. If it has been longer than that at your business, it's past time to begin. At the very least, it's important to revisit the assumptions (and their proofs) that support your company's strategy once a year. List all the assumptions that drive your business, along with a cursory check of your key competitors and their moves. For each, do enough homework every year to see if those assumptions are still valid in today's environment. That might mean as little as thirty to forty hours of research followed by a one-day off-site checkup with the leadership team.

If all the key assumptions are validated, most of leadership's focus can return to execution. However, if the environment has changed sufficiently to challenge those assumptions, then begin a deeper strategic planning process. At the end, create a list of key assumptions and other triggers so management knows what to watch out for on the horizon.

One type of trigger is a big competitor's investment in your sector. For example, Jamba Juice, a restaurant chain with more than 820 locations worldwide and system-wide revenues of $500 million, had focused on fruit-based smoothies for years while maintaining a small selection of fresh-squeezed carrot, orange, and wheat grass health juices. When Starbucks announced the acquisition of juice maker Evolution Fresh (which had a very health-oriented line of drinks based on vegetables and roots) in November 2011, it triggered a strategic reevaluation at Jamba. On the very day Starbucks announced the acquisition, Jamba CEO James White said, "We will adjust our strategy as needed."

Adjust they did. Long before Starbucks went to market with any new juice products, Jamba began testing new fresh juice blends that included beets, kale, ginger, and cucumber in stores in San Francisco, across the bay from its Emeryville headquarters. It also created a new store design that put these types of juices at the forefront, a test that expanded to sixty stores in 2013 (in California, New York, Florida, and Nevada), with many more expected in 2014.

Keeping up with a powerhouse like Starbucks will be tough, but Jamba won't enter the ring with an unexamined, outdated strategy.

Remember: the fact that you're thriving today does not mean your strategy—or your operations—will work tomorrow.

This is why we plan.

Your Guide to Strategic Planning

To contribute to the strategic planning process, a person needs to understand the big picture: industry trends, the competition, the underlying drivers of supply and demand, and more. Therefore, the only people who should participate in strategic planning sessions are those who are well-informed on these issues. This can be a problem when owners or board members are uninformed (often the case in closely held midsized businesses).

If you've got uninformed but powerful people to manage, select a smaller team to do the early strategic work, aiming to present options to the board and other stakeholders, supplying them with sufficient information to help them make an informed decision.

In most cases, the entire executive team should be involved in strategic planning. However, in businesses with less than

$20 million in revenue, I have found some members of the top team focused on internal matters almost exclusively. For example, the controller may be the highest finance executive in a closely held business, but may not know anything beyond accounting. The warehouse manager may have stepped up to VP of operations, but might still be focused on inventory, not on the competition's moves. These people are not helpful in strategic planning sessions, and often pull the conversation down into the weeds, where they are most comfortable.

Consequently, strategic planning requires the full contingent of outward-facing leadership: sales and marketing, product development, and perhaps board members who are active in the industry. (Remind the strategic planning group that the ideas discussed are not to be shared until a final decision has been made, and it has been decided what should be shared, and by whom. As I've noted, strategic thinking is distracting for most operational teams.)

Finding strategic direction takes much more than deep thinking and online research. It generally takes prototypes, experimentation, hands-on research, and more. Much of that work goes bust. What seemed like a good idea simply isn't. That's not a problem; it's why we do this. The real question is: How do we staff and support these efforts?

One $60 million IT firm had long powered its sales through online paid advertising. However, its competitors increasingly were using (and growing with) a direct marketing model in which ideal customers are identified and then contacted through a combination of e-mail, mail, and phone calls, and approached with general marketing tools such as online webinars. Testing and developing such a process would (and should) take at least six months. The IT firm knew it should explore it.

But its attempts to test an outbound sales methodology were aborted three times in four years. The first time, the leadership argued that its resources would be better deployed increasing the company's online advertising spending. Budgets were adjusted accordingly. The second time, the company suffered a service interruption that cost big money to fix. Sales slumped and the test was shut down. The last time, a leader was hired with a great deal of experience in outbound sales, but in his opinion the business didn't fund his budget adequately and he resigned after eight months.

To this day, the firm still doesn't know if identifying and targeting customers and then reaching out to them (as their competitors do) would pay off in growth. It is still dependent on paid Google ads for most of its revenues.

What has this firm been doing wrong? It hasn't been acting strategically. No matter the size of the business, resources can't be grabbed haphazardly; new ideas can't be pursued in an ad hoc fashion. The work of identifying the ideal strategy for a firm flows out of annual strategic reviews. These reviews should spawn projects with timelines, budgets, and leadership accountability. These decisions should be made while taking the needs of the core business into consideration, and then acted upon.

Ideally, the teams that focus on research and strategic development are dedicated; that is, that's all they do. Because they have no responsibilities to or accountability for the core business, they are less likely to get distracted by the day-to-day ups and downs that all businesses face. This is a critical point, as a common business failing, especially in midsized companies, is the neglect of the long-term in favor of the urgent. The urgency of the strategy development team should derive from its own deadlines and deliverables, not the business's.

Smaller midsized firms (under $100 million revenues) may not have sufficient staff to create this kind of separation. Executives and team members alike will have tasks and initiatives in both the core business and the strategic side. Here, it's especially critical to have specific deliverables with hard time frames. It is also important to have a CEO with the fortitude to resist grabbing the time and resources allocated to strategy to solve immediate problems, painful though they might be.

The best strategic ideas come to companies courtesy of open ears, not flapping gums. They begin by tabling any and all talk of solutions (*especially* the CEO's). Instead, they start by staring hard at the facts and realities that surround the company.

The best contribution top leaders can make toward a productive strategy session is asking good, hard, open questions such as these five:

1. What are our most successful competitors doing right?
2. Where is our market headed in three years, and who will win or lose as a result?
3. What is our position in the marketplace, and who are we envious of?
4. What will our current best customer's pain points be in three years?
5. What do we *assume* to be true (given our current strategies), and what are all the possible situations that might overturn those assumptions?

The CEO might pose these questions (and others) during a discussion, but she should then keep quiet (hard as that may be) until everyone has contributed. Long silences are good; they mean that people are thinking. As soon as a team knows the CEO has a favorite idea or concept, the team will tend to line up behind it, whether the team believes in it or not, whether the idea is well conceived or not.

The CEO's job really begins at the end of the session, when she must process the ideas and discussions and work toward building consensus around next steps. That may mean that some ideas get the green light and others do not. But ending a strategic session with a brainstormed list of ideas and nothing on how to take the next step will be frustrating for any team. Unless next steps are defined, brainstorming sessions are a waste of time. The session's outcome must be a series of hypotheses about the best path forward *and* plans to test them.

That's right: test them. While start-ups might be able to justify throwing caution to the wind in favor of speed to market, midsized firms most certainly cannot. They have too much to lose, and they should have sufficient time to de-risk ideas before trying to scale them.

So much money is wasted when leaders think something is a fact when, in fact, it's not. It's important to learn the vast difference between a new and untested idea that we believe is good (emphasis on believe) and a hypothesis (where we have done the homework to construct a business case that supports our opinion). And, in turn, a hypothesis is very different than proving something true through a series of tests or pilot studies.

Your Guide to Operational Planning

Unlike the strategic planning process, in which internally focused leaders can gum up the works, when it comes to operational planning everyone can and should play. The operational planning process begins with the output of the strategic planning process, so the CEO should have a clear idea of the business's direction for the year ahead. The CEO then drafts a top-level operational plan (on his own or working with one or two others). This draft is then shown to the top team (the leaders of each function) who then work on creating second-level plans, pulling in their support personnel as needed, and ultimately getting their second-level plans approved by the CEO. Once the functional plans are completed, the next level of management dives in to create departmental plans that support their function.

While there may be full meetings of the entire leadership team to kick off or wrap up the operational planning process, the real work is done in small groups, pounding out tactical details and coordinating with other departments and groups.

The plan-set is built in three phases:

Phase 1: Top-down drafts. The CEO's draft is created, then the functions', then the departments'.

Phase 2: Bottom-up feasibility. Work is done at all levels to verify budget, cross-department support, feasibility, and resource allocation. Plans are adjusted, and teams meet, starting from

The Three Phases of Plan Building

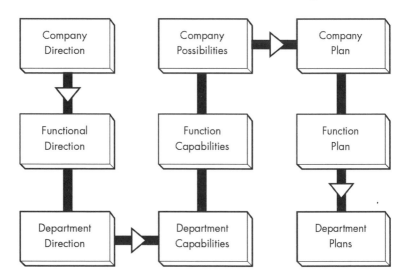

FIGURE 2-2: Building a plan set exclusively top down is a mistake; there is lots of essential knowledge at all levels. Likewise, letting the team lead the planning process and set the pace for the company is ill-advised. Good plan building is an iterative process.

the lower leadership levels to adjust targets and scope, and to assure that controlling plans are in fact the sum of their supporting plans.

Phase 3: Top-down final decisions. The CEO looks at the resulting plan-set and makes informed decisions about changes, including adding resources and adjusting priorities. Final decisions are made, and plans at all levels are adjusted and finalized.

Only the Best: When Ideas Compete

Both strategic and operational planning can produce a cornucopia of ideas. Actually, it's fairly easy to get a good idea. But no company has adequate time and resources to pursue all the good ideas. Instead, the company must identify the *best* ideas, and only work on those.

This is more easily said than done. Why? Because most of us think about the businesses we lead all the time. We think about them as we drive to work; we think about them before we fall asleep. When we wake up, a good idea pops into our heads and we want to see it come to life. The best CEOs (and entrepreneurs) are both imaginative and action oriented. Our good ideas keep coming, and we often think the new one is better than the last. But, hey, we've already spent a good slice of our R&D budget on that last idea. Should we stick with the first one, or consider those costs sunk and jump on our new epiphany?

That, of course, would depend on which idea is truly better. But how can we know? What should we do?

The answer is to make ideas compete. This entails being more deliberate about the process. We should follow these six steps to make sure we're investing in our best ideas:

1. Conduct a strategic session to determine the company's overall direction and its big-picture strategy. There is a strong

argument for focusing on your firm's core competencies; in the past, those strengths set you apart from your competitors. They may still. And new core competencies are hard to come by.

2. From that session, develop a list of possible ways to execute the strategy. Make sure you collect and list all the plausible ideas. This means much more than a single brainstorming session. It should be a careful competitive analysis that includes discussions with customers.

3. Spend a few hours digging into each idea, narrowing the list to perhaps a dozen or so. Make all the ideas compete with one another.

4. Write a business case (a rough proposal for action and an analysis of the likely results of that action) for each of the dozen, laying out the reasons for (and against) a likely return on investment. Depending on the risks, it might take twenty to forty hours to create each business case and take all but a few ideas off the table. Make all the remaining ideas compete with one another.

5. Narrow this list to three ideas you can both afford and execute properly. These will be your best ideas based on the needs and resources of your company.

And no, you're not done yet.
Create a testing program to *prove* that these ideas can succeed. These might be small regional market tests, bubblegum-and-tape prototypes to demo in front of key customers or even outsourcing the manufacture of a short-run of product to get a quick test completed. This reduces the risk of tinkering with your core strategy because these new ideas are vetted and tested *before* they are introduced (with great fanfare and significant investment) to the company at large.

Innovate Without Impeding Core Business Activities

FIGURE 2-3: Remember I mentioned earlier the freeway that represented your core business? When ideas compete to get on that freeway, and when they have an on-ramp that ensures they enter the core business at the speed of traffic, they are truly accretive to value.

Experimenting, Not Tinkering

Lori Bush, CEO of $250 million Rodan + Fields, a San Francisco–based skin care company selling through the direct sales channel, was facing inconsistent results in late 2009 from business development efforts across the country. While the salespeople (Rodan + Fields calls them consultants) loved the products, a high percentage struggled to sell enough to make a difference either to their own lives or to Rodan + Fields's top line.

Bush's sales leader wanted to continuously spike the company's commission plan with temporary short-term bonuses to encourage the consultants to put more oomph into their efforts. However, Bush worried that could attract consultants who "worked the compensation plan" and didn't care as much about the company mission of "changing skin and changing lives."

At the same time, Bush and industry adviser Oran Arazi-Gamliel became intrigued by a behavioral training method that might help low performers improve and identify future high performers. But the company's sales team was concerned about conducting a broad behavioral study in the field, arguing that it could become a distraction from the company's core business.

The question for Bush: Which idea—bonuses or training— would best serve its consultants and the company's future growth?

Bush believed that if the behavioral training worked, it would keep consultants more aligned with the company mission of changing lives (by supplementing the consultants' income) and changing skin (with the company's products). Still, she listened to her sales team's concerns, and allowed some testing of short-term incentive bonuses to see if they could spur sales in a sustainable fashion.

One sign that a CEO is tinkering with strategy is executive team resistance. Passionate CEOs often struggle to open their ears to the counsel of those around them, usually to their company's detriment. But in this case, Bush listened, and found a way to minimize both financial risks and the distraction factor.

In 2010 Bush and Arazi-Gamliel created a behavioral training pilot program. They identified some first-time consultants who were excelling. Then the two investigated the behaviors that led to those consultants' success. They tested training consultants on these identified behaviors in Atlanta. This had minimal impact on the core organization, and Arazi-Gamliel, an outside adviser with no operational responsibilities, ran the program.

By the end of 2010, Rodan + Fields's top line had grown to $22 million, some of it due to the incentive bonuses. But those top-line gains soon diminished when the bonus-enhanced compensation plan—which lacked profitability—was set back to normal levels. The bonuses weren't sustainable, and the program was wound down. However, the Atlanta behavioral training program had been a clear success, turning a stubbornly underdeveloped market into the top region in the United States. Sales leapt 300 percent in Georgia in the fall of 2010, and the gains continued into 2011. The firm has since replicated the process in numerous geographies across the U.S., including California, Texas, and Washington, D.C.

Had Bush launched the behavioral training campaign nationwide without testing, she would have consumed company resources and hurt the bottom line. Consequently, the training might not have been seen as successful as it in fact was. If she'd had her management team drive the pilot, rather than the independent Arazi-Gamliel, Bush certainly would have diverted her team's focus, and the top line might have suffered, again obscuring the results of the behavioral training program. Similarly, if she'd gone all-in on the rich commission program, the hit to the company's bottom line would have jeopardized its future, and perhaps led her to abandon the behavioral testing. In short, she would have reaped all the spoiled fruit of CEO strategy tinkering. But by testing carefully selected hypotheses in a low-risk manner, with minimal involvement of the core team, she mitigated each strategy's risks while pursuing new opportunities, the correct path for midsized firms.

Thanks to the behavioral training program, many consultants who might not have been able to stick with the company are now successful enough to boost their family incomes. The program also identified standouts with the ability to grow into high-performing regional leaders, a group critical to the company's overall growth.

By early 2012, the firm flew past the $100 million revenue mark and crossed the $200 million run rate by midyear 2013. Bush's carefully calibrated experiments with competing ideas didn't distract the firm from its core business. Instead, it helped to sort out the options and determine which idea was best.

That's testing, not tinkering. And it works.

Unsure about the difference between testing, tinkering, and valuable innovation? Employ the same diagnostics I use with my clients with this online assessment at www.ceotoceo.biz/mightytools.html. It will give you an idea of how seriously this silent growth killer is affecting your company.

A Simple Plan to Limit Tinkering

Most CEOs won't admit it, but oversight makes us better executives. The worst cases of strategic tinkering come from CEOs with complete freedom. A CEO I knew was in the trucking business. One of his customers made spaghetti sauces. It could never pay its bills, but it nevertheless persuaded the CEO that it had a big win in the offing. Despite the advice of a powerless advisory board, the CEO decided to acquire the sauce company. He invested hundreds of thousands. Six months later, the sauce company was out of business, and the trucking business's hard-won profits were gone.

A strong board might have reminded the CEO that his business was trucking, not sauce-making. Boards should act to require the CEO to stay within the firm's approved vision and mission. CEOs who understand how a strong, involved board can help them will make sure their boards are stocked with experience and talent.

Of all the C-suite executives, CFOs have the greatest chance to rein in a tinkering CEO. They are acutely aware of the effects of distraction and bad decisions on the financial statements. And it's the CFO's fiduciary responsibility to sound the alarm when targets are missed. Yet most CFOs won't sacrifice their relationship with the CEO (or their jobs) in the face of a chief executive who won't listen. In fact, almost no one (other than a strong board) can deal with a CEO who refuses to listen.

CFOs need to understand that they'll never be able to completely dissuade their CEO from tinkering, but even winning a 20 percent tinkering-reduction is a big win. CFOs should be persistent, and CEOs must remember to seek the CFO's advice and listen carefully. This will encourage the CFO to keep presenting his opinions, even if the CEO doesn't accept them all.

But CEOs can help curb their own tinkering impulse in a very simple way: by putting their vision for the company down on paper. *Writing it down makes it real.* (There, I've said it again.)

I sat down with more than one hundred CEOs and asked them what their company's most important priorities are. Generally, they quickly can outline the crucial key performance indicators (KPIs), the critical projects that must be executed, and the three to five differentiators that make their business thrive. Unfortunately, most have never shared their insights with their team in a concise written document.

These simple plans, often just one page, can create clarity and agreement. They promote focus, and make it easy for everyone to assess the company's performance and progress each month. As targets are missed and the team focuses on achieving them, it becomes increasingly intolerant of the tinkering that gets in the way of execution. And when the tinkering starts, the CEO will face a team that will be able to ask how the tinkering fits into the CEO's own written plan. And, if the new ideas are truly superior to those that preceded them, what parts of the original plan should be reprioritized?

This will stop many CEOs in their tracks as they remember the conviction with which they created and wrote down their plan in the first place. Again, even if this only stops 20 percent of the tinkering, it is still a major win.

Even at start-ups with relatively small leadership teams, being clear about the organization's priorities and what work should be done first is essential. Operating plans, progress tracking, and prioritization do not have to be bureaucratic or cumbersome. If the CEO is to be free to innovate, she must know that the rest of her team is getting the right things done each day. Yet planning and organization don't come naturally to many founder-CEOs, and that job falls to their senior leaders.

One of my clients was a self-acknowledged tinkerer. She loved spotting new opportunities and chasing them, and found running the core business to be boring. But she understood that building value in her own company required that she slow down her tinkering. In fact, she became so excited at the prospect of formal planning as a tool to limit her own tinkering that she made a large poster showing the company's one-page plan and posted it prominently on an office wall. She reasoned that if she started to tinker, it would be clear to everyone that she was violating her own plan.

So how can CEOs and their teams find the proper balance between strategic intransigence and the alluring temptations of tinkering? No CEO and no top team should ever stop thinking strategically. But they should keep such thoughts and discussions from the execution team. Top executives should be able to discuss strategy—and changes to it—without confusing it with or negatively affecting current execution priorities. For those leaders striving to promote a more transparent organization, produce a brief and very high-level summary after strategic off-sites, just enough to stop misunderstandings and supposition.

If the reconnaissance work to explore a new strategy requires more than discussion, a separate team should be assembled to do just that. And keep it low-key. Most strategic ideas that at first appear to be brilliant are discarded upon review and testing. It's best that this happens in the background until one new strategy rises to the level of a rollout.

Disciplined processes such as business planning and monthly reviews of the plans, combined with broad visibility throughout the firm, will also play a strong role in keeping tinkering at bay, and keeping midsized businesses the healthier for it.

3

Reckless Attempts at Growth

As you may have surmised from the previous chapter, tinkering with your strategy—especially when the tinkerer is tinkering at the top of the company—is not a good thing. As we've seen, what begins as tinkering can lead to a poorly considered strategic shift, which quickly can become a full-blown disaster. But midsized companies can still be vulnerable even when their new path for growth is well vetted. In the effort to scale, costs can balloon. And as they do, revenues can lag and cash, inevitably, runs dry. Slowly, the sense of hope and promise that informed the new strategy drains away and turns into dread.

That feeling of dread welled up in me at a 2013 Alliance of Chief Executives meeting when a CEO and member of the group presented his thinking on what I felt was a risky growth strategy. To be sure, he was beginning from a position of strength. His $300 million company was a cash machine with strong and accelerating profitability, mid-teens annual revenue growth and a dominant share of its market. Yet I had to wonder about the level of risk he was assuming as he gunned for faster growth. Did he really understand the breadth of those risks and whether they were worth it?

Growth always entails risk, and it usually costs money. If the attempt at growth costs too much and revenue doesn't match it, that bigger firm you're trying to become will not materialize. What does materialize is a cash crunch.

It's tempting for executives at midsized companies to believe, like the CEO at that meeting, that the only time they can run out of cash is when revenue is falling off a cliff. (See chapter 6, "The Liquidity Crash.") On the contrary, fast-growing midsized firms are just as susceptible to running out of cash as companies with declining revenue, perhaps even more so. Simply put, they can spend too much too fast, or spend too little too late. It's like a driver pulling into oncoming traffic to pass on a two-lane road: misjudging distance and speed can be fatal.

Unless management can capably gauge the speed with which both expenses and revenues are likely to grow over time, a midsized company gunning for growth faces the prospect of running out of money and all its ugly consequences, such as being forced to pull back on new product development or slash the sales force. Sure, these moves will preserve cash in a crunch. But they will also erode revenue over time, ultimately extending the cash drought. And then you can kiss your growth good-bye.

Reckless attempts at growth. This is the third silent killer of midsized company growth.

Money Can't (Always) Buy You Growth

The problem of properly calibrating spending in pursuit of growth is real and broad based. A clear majority of U.S. midsized companies surveyed in the third quarter of 2013 by Ohio State University and GE Capital were highly concerned about their costs. (OSU and GE Capital say the companies, which ranged in revenue from $10 million to $1 billion, are representative of midsized companies in the United States). When asked about their key challenges, 90 percent pointed to the cost of health care, 86 percent worried about the overall cost of doing business, and 84 percent complained about their ability to maintain margins.[1]

Hanging onto cash is critical for midsized companies. Driving the top line to offset the money you spend to grow isn't easy; survey respondents expected top line growth to fall from 5.5 percent in Q3 2013 to 4.4 percent in Q3 2014.

Examples abound of midsized companies that couldn't or didn't adjust the velocity of their spending in a timely fashion. When a giftware company merged with another company, its leaders were optimistic about its potential for growth as a larger player in the market and they were willing to spend to seize those opportunities. But they greatly underestimated the cost and time it took to integrate the acquired company. (See chapter 4, "Fumbled Strategic Acquisitions," for more on the challenges of growing by acquisition.) While the company's expenses mounted, integration hiccups irritated customers and hurt sales. Undercut by mounting customer defections and a deep industry downturn, the giftware company's revenue plunged 40 percent in one year.

The business continued to operate at a loss for another year as its leadership, ever hopeful that a higher top line was just around the corner, conducted business as usual. But its crumbling balance sheet grew less and less able to support the company's growing debt. When the company finally began to cut spending, it did so in a rush and cut muscle as well as fat. That reduced production and decreased billings.

The giftware company's downward spiral continues to this day, as it struggles to pay for purchases needed to fill orders. The growth it was gunning for never materialized and it's sinking deeper into debt. Thanks to the merger, it was a bigger business for a while, but it also was a less profitable one.

All midsized businesses should generate positive cash flow

for most of their existence. Only occasionally should management invest more cash than the business is generating, and that decision should *never* be made lightly. And there should be a clear path and timeline for when the business will be cash-flow positive.

This is too often forgotten in pursuit of growth.

CEOs hear about venture-backed start-ups that raise money round after round, investing it in programs that will scale first and become profitable (they hope) later. Amazon.com is often presented as an example of a business that spent its way to growth and its current immensity, apparently heedless of generating positive cash flow. That makes for great news stories. In certain circumstances, it can be a viable strategy for early-stage businesses. But face it: most midsized businesses are not Twitter or Facebook and never will be. They have owners who want a return on their investment, month after month, year after year.

This means that for most midsized businesses, losing money is unacceptable *under any circumstances.*

Businesses that stay strong in all economies and survive bad times are very disciplined about this. I recently left the office of a client whose CEO was upset and eager to take action because his profit margins had fallen from 6 percent to 4 percent without (in his opinion) an acceptable reason. His company wasn't even losing money yet. It is this discipline that keeps companies out of a liquidity crisis.

On the other hand, when growth initiatives go bad and cash flow goes negative, CEOs and the boards of midsized companies deal with it in many ways, and some of them are dysfunctional. Feeling that everything they have is at stake, they act to defend what they have and become intensely, even overly, frugal. But by failing to invest in new products, marketing, sales, and technology, they end up allowing cash-rich competitors to gain market share. Often, they never catch up. Instead of growing, the business contracts and, over time delivers less cash to its owners. More aggressive CEOs will try to spend their way out of failed growth initiatives, believing (or just hoping) that cash inflows eventually will increase. But they always know they are making a judgment call, and most lose sleep over it.

If a big growth initiative is in your plans for the year ahead, take this online assessment at www.ceotoceo.biz/mightytools.html to learn just how much sleep you should be losing, or how much work you must do before you start spending.

Three Elements of Sound Decision Making

From my research and consulting experience, I have found three elements that go into sound decision making when cash flow goes negative while you're gunning for growth. Getting to the heart of these issues increases the odds of achieving both growth and positive cash flow:

1. **Market predictability.** Will sufficient demand exist for your product when you need it? How can you be sure?

2. **Execution confidence.** Will your team be able to build the product and capture the sales at the level you require when you require it? What is your confidence level?

3. **Forecasting acumen.** Are the pro forma financial statements comprehensive and accurate? If the market is there and the team executes the plan, will the actual financial results match the pro forma? How much of your net worth are you willing to bet on it?

Assuming excellent forecasting acumen (a big assumption), spending velocity should be determined as follows:

Optimal Spending Velocity

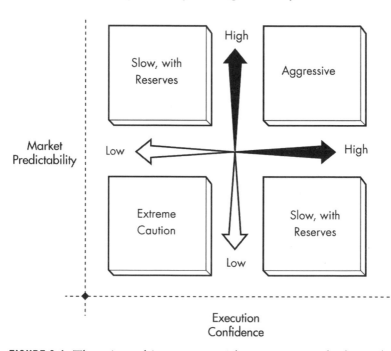

FIGURE 3-1: There is nothing wrong with operating in the lower left (high risk) quadrant. Just don't bet too much! But if you're certain you're in the upper right quadrant, a heavy bet may be indicated to grab market share and growth. Know your quadrant, and proceed appropriately.

But, oh, if only it were as easy as the chart makes it look. Most CEOs pursuing growth believe passionately in their vision and mission, often to a fault. They believe the market is more predictable than it turns out to be. They have unbounded (and all too often unfounded) confidence in their team's ability to execute. Not surprisingly, unpleasant surprises pop up that they didn't account for in the pro forma.

Here's how to mitigate the impact of those inevitable surprises.

Get Out of Your Office

To competently assess market demand, the CEO and his top team must get out of their offices and into their marketplace. Trade shows and industry association meetings are excellent venues for meeting other businesspeople and asking them questions about your market. Customer visits are invaluable. With your customers' permission, you should record their responses to a standard set of questions (asked conversationally) and then look for patterns.

You can gain further insights about your marketplace by tracking competitors and measuring objective indicators of their success. For industries large enough to be followed by research firms (such as Gartner in the technology sector), plenty of secondary data is available. Regular meetings with investment bankers who study your industry will yield more information. Remember: new data trumps old data; what you learned last year may not be relevant today.

But investigating the marketplace is not the CEO's job alone. Every member of the top team and the sales and marketing departments should be collecting this information as a matter of course. In particular, the CFO should be informed and involved, as he will be the ultimate architect of the financial forecast. Letting the management team—not just the CEO and CFO—gather and jointly discuss this market data will greatly reduce the chances that a company will spend money on growth based simply on the biases, predispositions, hunches, and gut feelings of the top few leaders. Leaders tend to be optimistic. Optimism is good, but unless it's informed, it can be dangerous.

Still, I put far more trust in the forecasts of executives who have a stake in a business than I do in those who work only for wages, however generous. (Venture capital firms operate this way, usually insisting that all top executives hold stock.) Executives with an ownership position have much more to lose if they under- or overaggressively estimate demand.

However, midsized companies are established enterprises, not start-ups, and so distributing equity is a little trickier. I'm not suggesting changing your ownership structure right away. But as your executives weigh in on the state of your marketplace and the company's ability to compete in it, you must consider the source. Those with real skin in the game (even as a significant element of their long-term incentive compensation) are much more likely to strive to forecast accurately.

Understanding Your Market

Taking a more complete measure of its market helped BlueArc, a venture-backed data storage equipment manufacturer, build a cash reserve despite having to make large, risky investments to grow in turbulent times. In 2008 BlueArc's CFO, Rick Martig, was worried: cash flow from operations had turned negative as the Great Recession began. Because Martig and BlueArc's other executives had been getting out of their offices and into the company's fast-changing marketplace, they had a gut feeling that to grow they needed to add a mid-priced product to complement their high-end, high-performance product portfolio. This would require R&D investment even as cash from ongoing operations was dwindling.

But a gut feeling, even backed by BlueArc's intelligence gathering, wasn't quite enough. Fortunately, several of BlueArc's larger competitors had started down the path to IPO or were eventually acquired, so their financial and operating results suddenly became visible and there was a premium building for a BlueArc business model in the market. Their financial data reinforced BlueArc's belief that it needed that mid-priced product. On the strength of all those inputs, BlueArc raised $7 million in venture debt, which enabled it to complete the R&D work to design, produce, and bring the product to market. At the same time, the company cut G&A expenses and even some of its sales staff. Still, the senior team knew it needed more cash to continue investing in the business, and it raised another $21 million.

BlueArc's new product became a major success. That enabled it to hit its targets and get it to breakeven in EBITDA eighteen months later. As it prepared for its own IPO in 2011 (by that time, BlueArc's revenue was $86 million), it was acquired by Hitachi Data Systems at a very good revenue multiple.

BlueArc took a big risk. It decided to grow by developing a new product, borrowing the money to do so even as its own revenues were declining in the middle of an economic downturn. Scary. But, actually, it was an informed, thoughtful risk because the company knew its market and its competitors.

I'm sure you work to assess your marketplace. But have you ever been caught by surprise when sales spiked up or spiraled down? Have you introduced new products or run promotional campaigns with results very different than those you were expecting? If so, you should seriously examine the processes you employ for understanding your market. Unlike the caveat your broker adds when he's pitching a stock or fund, past results in assessing your market are, in fact, a strong indicator of future performance.

Making a market assessment such as BlueArc did, and having enough confidence in it to invest significant resources and assume significant debt on the strength of that assessment, takes time, commitment, guts, and humility. Yes, humility. There are no sure things in life or in business. But some owners and CEOs of midsized companies feel invincible. They've been successful; obviously they know their market, and they don't think they need to do further research. And some of their sales leaders are equally sure of their market expertise and don't want to take time away from selling to validate what their gut tells them.

But key to knowing when and when not to invest for growth, in times both good and bad, is making market assessment an ongoing process. Once that is part of your company's DNA, all your forecasts and decisions will be far better informed.

No matter how long you've been in a particular market, no matter how well you think you know it, your gut is just not reliable. You might be correct, but the risk of failure is too high, and it could well take you two or three adjustments to get it right. Reserving enough cash to finance several attempts to bring in new revenue is the best approach. And step one in gauging how much cash you should spend in pursuit of growth is getting clear on the state of your market and doing everything you can to improve the accuracy of your predictions.

So You Think You Can Execute?

How likely is it that your team will deliver the results you expect? How likely is it that they will deliver them on time? Look back at our Optimal Spending Velocity chart. Low execution confidence—even in a highly predictable market—demands that you proceed slowly and keep extra financial reserves on hand.

Too often, even when executive teams have less than complete confidence in their company's ability to execute, they are loath to adjust their expectations. The growth goal is too tempting, too exciting. Now, adrenaline-fueled excitement works on the football field; it can lead an underdog to victory over a powerhouse squad. But in businesses, it can convince us to spend more than we should.

To objectively calculate the odds that you will be able to execute your growth strategy effectively, ask yourself if you possess these five elements of execution success:

1. **A proven team.** A proven team is one that has worked together before and has recently succeeded on a similar project. With the learning curve and team-bonding risks out of the way, such a team can bring great energy and focus to the task at hand. A team whose individuals don't have work experience relevant to the role they will be playing (even if they are quick learners) cannot be considered proven. Similarly, if the individuals have not worked together before, there is a risk that the team will not gel.

2. **A realistic budget.** While major successes have been financed on a shoestring, and great growth opportunities have emerged from skunk works, underfunded efforts fail more often than not. The reasons for this are multiple. Salaries are too low to attract top talent. The vendors selected are not top-shelf. And even if you do attract high-quality partners, they'll place a lower priority on your project if they've had to make large pricing concessions. To conserve cash, we take shortcuts like sacrificing testing time or product quality. Shortcuts add risks to any growth initiative, risks you neither need nor want.

3. **Strong partners.** It makes sense to outsource aspects of a project that lie outside your core competency. Yet along with outsourcing's benefits (such as lower overhead, greater expertise, and perhaps a sharper focus on execution) comes the risk that your partners just won't perform. Often, they don't. The ideal partner should need your project to succeed as much as you do. If that's the case, they will fight through obstacles and strive to keep you happy. Ideally, the partner you choose will have executed successfully many similar projects and be financially and technically strong.

4. **Tested, proven processes.** Assumptions are the enemy of good execution, and testing is your secret weapon against

them. Kicking off a growth project that will devour significant budget without establishing at least some testing is risky, if not downright reckless. At the very least, test the sales process with one or two people, even on a part-time basis. Perform small-scale testing in a development environment. Draft several training protocols and test them on a few people.

5. **Low technical risks.** Technology can be a barrier to block competitors, assuming we have surmounted the same barrier ourselves. But delivering on a technological breakthrough is seldom easy. Firm leaders must listen carefully to the concerns of those performing the technical work. CEOs with too much confidence in their ability to figure things out can prevent real concerns from being aired. Trust your experts to identify obstacles, and listen to them. Strong oversight is required to confirm the level of risk. Ultimately, testing is your final proof.

A Failure to Execute

A toy importer in pursuit of growth needed to automate its warehouse to enter a new market. But, with predictable consequences, it ignored the five pillars of execution success.

First, it placed an executive with no systems integration experience in charge of implementing its warehouse automation system. He was helped by the company's in-house IT guy. They combined to form an unproven team. The company, tight on cash, didn't want to spend money on outside experts, so it did not have a strong partner (any partner, really) and the budget for the project was too small and, as it turned out, unrealistic. The company decided not to run parallel systems because it wanted the change implemented in time for its peak season. Therefore, the system was unproven and untested. Not surprisingly, the cutover was a month late and it still failed. As a result, it triggered massive shipping delays, a pileup of excess inventory, a gaggle of squawking customers who refused to pay, millions in losses and, ultimately, a full-blown liquidity crisis.

The fact that they failed was unfortunate, but you could hardly call it a surprise. Recklessly gunning for growth, the company shot itself in the foot. (For more on the travails of this company, and how it fell victim to all the growth killers, see the Conclusion, "Becoming a Mighty Midsized Company," page 189.)

Once growth is achieved, the execution story doesn't end. In fact, it may just be beginning. One big point of failure for midsized companies in pursuit of growth occurs when the business succeeds, and in succeeding outgrows its management team and its processes. We see it happen again and again. An Internet retailer gets overconfident at the first signs of successful growth. It doesn't have receivables or inventory that absorb cash as the business grows so it throws money at ad spending to get big fast without careful testing (which can take months to do properly). That just wastes dollars it will need later. And when later comes, and the money's not there, we read about the CEO stepping down, followed soon by the rest of his management team as the press piles on, writing that the management team was unprepared to run the company it had started. Think Groupon.

Long before a company begins gunning for growth it must carefully begin to scale its leadership team, infrastructure, and processes. (I'll delve into this in the last chapter.) Just as you'd train for a marathon, planning and training for a sharp uptick has to be done in advance of the need. Otherwise, you run the risk of your team dropping out of the race by the fifth mile with twenty-one more to go.

Forecasting Fundamentals

It is not enough to have a marketplace ready to buy, and a great team that can get the job done. We also must predict the future with enough specificity to plan in detail so we have what we need when we need it. When you're gunning for growth, it isn't safe to spend according to plan if the plan itself is flawed.

Forecasting is difficult. Most of the time, projects take longer than we expect them to, cost more, and are full of surprises. That's life. Not accounting for life is bad forecasting. Even if the project exceeds forecast, and sales are higher than expected, unplanned success can bring its own set of problems such as working capital stress, materials shortages, a suboptimal customer experience, and a management team that doesn't have the skills to run a bigger business.

Effective forecasting provides the opportunity to strike bargains with the external parties we will need for success. That can include investors, public markets, suppliers, and contract manufacturers. If you want to gain their trust and access their resources the next time you come to the table—and, of course, you do—you must deliver on your promises and hit your targets.

If you are likely to miss your forecast, you must reserve more cash to handle the surprises—enough to make a second try. So what are the best predictors of forecasting acumen? Here are five:

1. **Past performance.** If your company previously has been successful at forecasting, there is a strong likelihood it has acquired that competency—providing that most of the people who were successful before are still on board. Also, look to the kind of forecasts they succeeded in making. Forecasts for a line extension or even a new product can be difficult. But they're not nearly as complex as those needed for ambitious growth initiatives such as a large acquisition or developing a new business unit in an adjacent market. And if the past forecasting performance of your company is poor, you should put your growth plans on hold until you figure out why.

2. **Past performance of the CFO.** While many people will provide input for your forecast, there is one person who drives it. In a midsized company, that's usually the CFO. That person's track record is crucial. It takes experience for a CFO to learn where slippage usually occurs. Experience tells the CFO where the surprises lurk. Additionally, and most important, experience teaches the CFO to include the costs and items that inevitably make an impact on the forecast but are often overlooked.

Creating the forecast is only the first step. Staying on forecast requires an active financial manager who not only monitors what has happened but projects what is going to happen in the near future. Having such a CFO on the team (or hiring one) significantly increases the accuracy of your forecasting, provided this person is not overruled too often by the CEO or sidelined to irrelevancy.

3. **Past CEO commitment to hitting forecasts.** Companies often miss forecasts because the CEO gets "creative" and goes off plan. Maybe the CEO decides that the company's priorities have shifted. Maybe the CEO panics when things go off the rails and starts looking for other solutions. In some cases, the CEO just does not like the discipline of sticking to plan.

It is true that circumstances sometimes call for change. Yet this implies that the management team was unable to foresee that possibility when the forecast was created and failed to budget for it. This can be just as bad as undisciplined spending or insufficient sales. Wall Street certainly punishes public firms for missing forecasts, whatever the root cause.

A CEO can singlehandedly cause the company to miss its forecast. Looking at past behavior in this area is critical to assessing the probability of hitting the next one.

4. **The number and clarity of fallback plans.** It is naïve to think that the path to hitting a forecast is a straight line.

Management usually must make course corrections along the way. In a midsized firm, those adjustments must come early, before too much damage (overspending, missing critical milestones) has been done. Good forecasters identify the areas of risk up front and create triggers that kick off backup plans to stay on target. The presence of triggers—written and understood by all—increases the likelihood of staying on forecast.

In the case of storage manufacturer BlueArc, its CFO saw that it was coming off a poor quarter (revenue down close to 50 percent) during the 2008 economic crisis. The leadership team knew it needed to make some tough cuts. But it didn't cut in areas needed to develop the next-generation product that was critical to the company's growth strategy. Instead, it built a longer-term plan around preserving cash, focusing on delivering the new product, and only adding more salespeople as economic conditions improved. And the leadership made a commitment to the board that it would make further cuts if the company didn't achieve its revenue and profit milestones. The ability to keep that focus was critical to BlueArc's eventual acquisition by Hitachi Data Systems.

5. **Understanding the consequences.** The stock market swiftly punishes public companies that fail to meet forecast. As a result, these companies pour time and effort into setting realistic benchmarks, and they fight hard to achieve them. Yet in many private midsized companies, missed forecasts are met with a shrug of the shoulders. There are no consequences for poor forecasters.

In fact, in midsized companies there is often more pressure to agree to an overly optimistic forecast than there is to achieve it. This is a mistake of great consequence. Pressure to perform is a critical factor in all business operations. Setting the expectation that missed forecasts will be considered failures and delineating serious consequences for those failures will increase your likelihood of designing and hitting achievable forecasts. And if you have confidence in your forecast, you can gun for growth and spend more money more aggressively. If you do not, you must hold more cash in reserve so that you can recover from surprises.

Spending too much too fast can leave a company dead in the water, with no money for a second chance at success and a track record that won't impress any new funding sources. On the other hand, spending too cautiously when a strong growth opportunity exists often surrenders that opportunity to competitors.

Before you make a significant bet on growth, invest the time and effort necessary to understand your market thoroughly. Evaluate your team's ability to execute realistically, and assess its forecasting acumen rigorously. Then decide on what your spending velocity should be, and what level of risk you can assume prudently.

Doing otherwise can only be deemed reckless.

4

Fumbled Strategic Acquisitions

Not all mothers should let their sons grow up to be cowboys (or so advised Waylon Jennings and Willie Nelson), and not all CEOs should want their midsized firms to grow up to become Fortune 500 behemoths. But those who are eager to grow in leaps and bounds usually require more than organic growth to get there. They need the added revenue that comes from buying another company.

Good acquisitions can turbocharge growth. They can inject new vitality into moribund businesses. In fact, midsized companies often find it less expensive to buy another company—a competitor or a player in a new market—than to expand organically.

In the last decade, for instance, United Site Services, a Westborough, Massachusetts-based provider of portable toilets founded in 1999, grew into a national leader by buying a bigger platform company in a new metropolitan area and then a series of smaller competitors in the same region, eventually dominating the local market. The company repeated this strategy in new markets—buy the bigger player first, then scoop up the smaller guys—and in so doing expanded to twenty-three states and built a $120 million business from scratch before selling itself to a national firm.

Had United Site Services tried to launch portable toilet rental businesses in market after market, it would have taken far longer to get big if, indeed, it ever would have. The company would have faced entrenched competition in every market and a steep learning curve in every region. No way could United have gone from zero revenue in 2000 to $120 million in just three years.

But an acquisition can help you avoid all those challenges. It lets you cut to the front of the line. That's how TriNet Group, a San Francisco Bay Area–based provider of HR services to corporations, has more than doubled its revenue since 2009. Founded in 1988, the company grew to $100 million by 2009 through organic growth and several small acquisitions. But in 2009 it decided to go for turbo-growth. It bought a similar-sized competitor with a different customer base, Gevity HR, for nearly $100 million. The acquisition of the Florida-based company enabled TriNet to more than double its revenue (to $220 million) and become a market leader. And TriNet has been making acquisitions ever since.

Acquisitions are especially advantageous to midsized companies in shrinking markets where rivals are killing each other in profit-robbing price wars. Those wars reduce the funds available for innovation, making growth even more difficult. In such an environment, a midsized business can burn through capital just trying to survive.

Investing that capital by buying a competitor is a move that could be healthy for both buyer and seller. Acquisitions can open doors to new markets that are often closed to midsized companies due to a lack of talent or technology, and they can boost value in other ways. In the early 2000s, for instance, Internet search engine Ask Jeeves was a midsized firm in a market that was being overwhelmed by Google. Ask Jeeves made dozens of acquisitions before it was sold to IAC in 2005 for $1.8 billion.

So it's simple, right? If you want growth, just buy it. Not exactly. Sadly, acquisitions are risky. Mergers (of all sizes) are financially successful less than half the time, according to a 2003 Federal Trade Commission study.[1] In other words, the odds of acquisition success are worse than a coin toss. In most cases, revenue growth declines post-merger for both buyers and sellers.

That's why fumbling a strategic acquisition is the fourth silent growth killer of midsized organizations.

Midsized Firms, Outsized Risk

Many factors separate acquisition success from failure. And for the midsized firm, each factor is important because the odds of success are so poor and the stakes are so high. A Fortune 500 company can write off the loss of a failed acquisition and move on. But bad deals often derail midsized firms, and sometimes even kill them.

Where do acquisitions go wrong? The trouble for the midsized company often becomes visible in the integration phase (which is way too late), when the buyer's and the seller's operations and managements need to become one. As the acquirer invests more capital to make the deal work, and the ROI is not forthcoming, the company turns back to its core business. The acquired firm is starved of investment and attention and, like a plane running out of fuel, its engine sputters. But don't be too quick to blame the integration effort. Some acquisitions are simply destined to fail for a host of reasons.

Sometimes management doesn't realize it has made the wrong acquisition until it's too late. After it signs the paperwork, the top team of the acquiring company discovers products that were not as profitable as they were led to believe. Promising technologies in development are revealed to have major flaws. Sometimes the team realizes (too late) that they don't have the bandwidth or budget to handle a complicated integration.

Sometimes, the purchase price was just too high to begin with, the debt too burdensome. Sometimes a clash of cultures wears on the marriage. As both sides argue over the "way we've always done it here," valuable employees defect, taking their knowledge with them.

Still other acquisitions go bad due to geographic miscalculations. Consider the three food manufacturers a private equity firm rolled up in 2009. Their facilities were one thousand miles apart, which made the integration of operations and infrastructure almost impossible, thereby eliminating the economies of scale the purchaser thought to secure. Eighteen months later, the new, rolled-up company filed for Chapter 11.

Inadequate due diligence is a root cause of M&A disasters. A toy importer I know of grew irritated when a former customer—a retailer—became a competitor and it decided to fight back by buying another retailer. But the importer's CEO did not want his other customers to see him as a potential competitor so he wanted to keep the deal quiet and consequently did little due diligence on the retailer he was buying.

Surprise! The retailer was not as profitable as he thought it was. It took two years to turn it around. By that time, the importer had spent millions—all unanticipated—that amounted to an additional 50 percent over the original cost of the acquisition.

Obviously, acquiring the wrong company is painful. And yet, sometimes the target company *is* the right company, but the acquiring firm just isn't prepared to make the deal work. When that happens, the results are just as ugly. The big lesson: avoid buying the wrong firm in the first place.

Integration Execution: A Key to Success

While the average multibillion-dollar corporation has a deep bench of executives, most midsized companies run with very lean executive teams. But acquisitions are complex and require enormous amounts of attention. For this reason, acquisitions can stretch the management of a midsized company beyond the breaking point.

Of course, a distracted management team is one thing; money pouring out the door is another. The total cost of an acquisition is *always* more than the purchase price—in some cases, much more. Almost every acquisition involves legal and other advisory fees. But what many CEOs don't prepare for are the costs of integrating the acquired company.

The integration process is a key factor behind many failed acquisitions. In fact, every other aspect about a deal could be favorable—the target firm could be a perfect strategic fit; the acquirer's management team could have sufficient bandwidth; capital may be plentiful—but if you don't get the integration right, the acquisition will be a bust. And, realistically, you only get one bite at that apple, one opportunity to merge two often disparate cultures, processes, systems, and product lines into one.

So why, exactly, do integrations fail? Like everything else about acquisitions, it's complicated. When they go bad in larger midsized firms ($300 million to $1 billion), it is often due to a disconnect between the deal makers and the deal integrators. The top team conducts pre-close negotiations and then leaves the specifics of merging the two firms to the operating executives. However, the operating executives often have little say over the resources, commitments, and support they need even though they are expected to deliver the benefits of the deal that the top team promised the board.

Another reason that acquisitions fail in the integration phase is that the original purpose of the deal is forgotten over time. Integrations can take months or even years to complete. During this time, both the acquiring and acquired teams can lose track of the overarching acquisition strategy and become distracted by short-term issues. When the board or the CEO asks why the acquisition failed—which, again, happens at least 50 percent of the time—they often discover that the operating unit executives didn't stay focused on the original premise of the acquisition.

While integration is a key point of failure, acquisitions backfire for many other reasons. And, unfortunately, you are not likely to get highly actionable advice from the many investment bankers and consulting firms that pile up huge fees for guiding companies on big acquisitions. The hard truth is that you and your deal may well be their meal ticket. Consequently, your interests and theirs may not be aligned. Few will advise you to walk away from a deal—any deal.

Traditional M&A Advice Isn't Much Help

Good advice on integrating midsized companies after a merger is sorely lacking. The majority of books and articles on acquisition strategies concentrate on deal making: matching buyer and seller and closing the deal. Even my own book *The Feel of the Deal*[2] focused on connecting with the seller and wrapping up the deal, not integrating the business (although it remains one of the few texts to address midsized-company acquisitions). And those books that don't focus on getting the deal done are devoted mainly to exit strategies: how the owners of a company can sell their business for a premium price. These books aren't about how to increase the odds that a strategic acquisition will work.

As for the M&A experts, just about every large consulting and accounting firm publishes white papers, reports, and surveys on M&A strategy. Virtually all of this material is aimed at companies with at least $1 billion in revenue. Take Big Four accounting firm KPMG's 2009 study, *The Determinants of M&A Success,* frequently cited by journalists, scholars, and corporate development experts. The average deal size examined was $3.4 billion, and very little of the content addresses M&A success in the most critical and complicated areas: properly selecting targets, creating integration strategies, and laying the groundwork for making acquisitions.[3]

Consequently, the CEOs of midsized companies adopt the best-practice advice given to large enterprises but then find it difficult to implement.

Why? In making acquisitions, midsized companies, compared with large companies, face two fundamental handicaps:

1. Most big companies have enormous financial depth. They have giant cash reserves and public market stock they can pay with. And, as they are usually acquiring companies that are much smaller than they are, the vast majority of their acquisitions won't kill their growth even if they end up writing them off entirely. By contrast, midsized firms typically acquire companies that are closer to their own size. For example, many $50 million firms can find targets with between $5 million and $25 million in revenues, all of which, if mishandled, will materially affect their profits. And few sellers want illiquid private company stock as payment.

2. Most big companies create teams that spend all their time analyzing and integrating acquisitions. These deal teams can range from thirty to one hundred people—more than the entire head count at many smaller midsized companies. Merging two companies takes a great deal of managerial bandwidth, something often in shorter supply in midsized than in larger companies. Midsized companies seldom can dedicate full-time staff to deal sourcing, deal making, and integration. That wouldn't make sense, as in most cases they do far fewer deals with far less frequency than large companies.

Having less financial strength and less M&A expertise and focus means that strategic acquisitions are fundamentally different for midsized acquirers, which is why advice designed for big companies doesn't work for midsized firms.

How to Beat the Odds

I've spent the last two years, while writing this book, studying midsized company acquisitions, successful and unsuccessful. I've talked with executives and former executives at more than fifty midsized companies that took the bold step of buying growth (or, at least, what they thought would be growth). From our discussions, I saw that the successful acquisitions all involved these four best practices:

1. Buying only companies that enhance the core strategy of the business
2. Adding staff with M&A experience long before the deal closes
3. Carefully assessing whether a potential deal is the right size and the company a strong fit culturally and operationally
4. Having a disciplined, focused integration process

Let's explore each practice.

Making Sure an Acquisition Supports a Core Strategy

Midsized firms are asking for trouble when they acquire a firm that is not central to their core strategy. I understand how this can happen. An investment banker alerts you to a company for sale (perhaps one of his clients), a deal that's "just too good to pass up." It could be in a fast-growing sector. It could be grossly underperforming in a slow-growing sector and simply needs better management.

Such thinking is dangerous. Acquiring companies is not a strategy. Acquisitions must *support* a strategy: geographic expansion, talent acquisition, diversification into an adjacent business, vertical integration by buying a synergistic customer or vendor, product diversity, competitor neutralization, scale, and so on. If you acquire a company that doesn't help you execute your core strategy, it's as if you are wandering through a flea market because you need a side table but you get sidetracked and buy ten other items, none of which is a side table. Two weeks later, you're staring at an odd collection of items in your living room, wondering why you still don't have a side table. You got sidetracked.

Don't let an investment banker or business owner sidetrack you. When an acquisition isn't fully in line with your firm's core strategy, you will inevitably starve it of the resources it needs to grow because your core business will always be more important to you.

But when an acquisition initiative emerges from a strategic planning process, supporting and investing in it is synonymous with executing your core strategy. (See chapter 2, "Strategy Tinkering at the Top," page 44, for the fundamentals of strategic planning.) It thus is more likely to gain your organization's full support. This M&A philosophy—buying only companies that help a firm execute its core strategy—helped grow EORM, a San Jose, California–based environmental, health, safety (EHS), and sustainability consulting firm founded in 1990. Until 2010, the seventy-five-person, $13 million–revenue company had shunned acquisitions. But in recent years, growth had stalled and top managers decided they needed to include acquisitions as a part of their growth strategy.

EORM created clear guidelines for acquisition targets. They

had to be companies performing the same or related EHS and sustainability consulting services. They had to be small (with ten to twenty employees), and based either in Southern California or the East Coast (to support geographic expansion).

EORM launched a disciplined search following those criteria. The first deal on the East Coast fell through in late 2010 but the firm acquired a second target company, Sigma Engineering, in Southern California, in August 2011. EORM now has a critical mass in a target geography, and penetration in two new sectors (corporate retail and public sector) as well as new skills in important service areas such as environmental site assessments and remediation. That acquisition has also helped boost both companies' fortunes. Since then, EORM has grown to 175 employees and $27 million in revenues in 2013, and it is continuing to include acquisitions in its growth with a second acquisition targeted for 2015.

But what about diversification? While that is important for many Fortune 500 companies, diversification can be deadly for the midsized firm. Most midsized companies have neither the finances nor the managerial bandwidth to turn around a business they don't thoroughly understand.

Remember that trucking company I mentioned in chapter 2? Its management learned this sober truth the hard way. The company had been growing slowly but steadily in a low-margin business. In 2003 a big customer (a sauce manufacturer) got into financial trouble. The trucking company's CEO got involved in the nasty task of collections, but found the manufacturer and its products intriguing. He sensed an opportunity. The manufacturer offered the business to him at a low price, and he thought the deal was too good to pass up. But soon after he bought the business, complications arose. It needed capital and good management. The CEO swooped in, bringing his management team with him. But they had day jobs and were stretched thin. Six months later, the CEO shut down the sauce company and walked away from his investment after losing $370,000.

Midsized companies thrive when their strategy is highly focused, clear, and well executed every day. But determining whether an acquisition is aligned tightly with your strategy is not a simple problem to solve. The answer lies in how the acquisition helps you grow your existing business. The more it does, the more you can tolerate a risky or complex deal. You should be able to answer "Yes" to these three questions:

1. Is the acquisition essential to your firm's strategy?
2. Are you certain that your firm will be more financially successful because of this acquisition?
3. If the acquisition requires 30 percent more effort and capital than you think it might, would you still do it?

If your answer to any of these questions is no, you should walk away from the deal. Save your powder for a more worthy target.

Having M&A Expertise on Staff

Can you imagine performing a heart transplant with no training or experience? Of course not. But making an acquisition for the first time is not that much easier. Both are complex activities where a living organism is involved. Yet M&A rookies operating with little guidance often lead midsized company acquisitions.

A giftware company (mentioned briefly on page 65) found this out, again the hard way. It bought another giftware business but neither management team had any acquisition experience. The negotiation was difficult, but the buying team was eager. It had outside legal counsel, an investment bank, and an accounting firm backing it up. It should have been set, right? However, it failed to understand the lease obligations to exit one of acquired firm's facilities, underestimating shutdown costs by hundreds of thousands of dollars. This crucial overhead cost reduction had to wait, absorbing working capital needed to grow the firm. Slowing cash flow angered suppliers (who were paid late) and customers (who were served more slowly). New product development (starved of cash) stalled. Two years after the acquisition, the giftware firm continued to struggle under a heavy debt load and with weak sales.

So where was the legal counsel? The accounting firm? The investment bank? Why didn't they help the firm avoid this disastrous acquisition? Because all three external advisers' expertise was in finding deals and getting them done. They were not focused on helping management find the right company, or assessing how easily it could be integrated, or planning and executing the integration. For that, midsized companies need to rely on their own resources. And they better have them.

Having executives with M&A integration experience on staff is critical. And they need to have been there for a while to understand the company's culture and possess the relationships throughout the organization that let them call on the company's human resources. Renting this expertise from accounting and consulting firms is problematic, even at those larger midsized firms that can afford it. Rented experts don't know the culture of the acquiring company and lack authority to make decisions. Generally, they are not domain experts either, and often fail to bring much more to the table than checklists and project management skills. Certainly, that can be helpful. But they don't bridge the M&A experience gap.

Integrating an acquisition was part of the job description of the corporate development team at CCC Information Services. The Chicago-based company provides software and services for automobile insurance claims. When Tom Baird (SVP of corporate strategy and development) ran the corporate development team in 2004 (the company had revenue of about $200 million), he had two employees: a senior staffer focused on deal sourcing and a junior staffer who did financial modeling. When an acquisition was in the offing, he pulled together a team of executives from HR, legal, accounting, and other departments. And Baird himself was an old hand at acquisitions, with nineteen years of M&A leadership at large corporations (TRW and Reynolds and Reynolds) prior to CCC.

But you don't have to be a $200 million company to have some M&A expertise in-house. Smaller companies that want to acquire are still big enough to dedicate people to the task. When Lyndon Faulkner became CEO of equipment case manufacturer Pelican Products in 2005, he believed the firm (with revenue of $80 million at the time) had to grow through acquisition. While he was the only executive at Pelican with M&A experience, he had plenty of it. So he mentored his team through the acquisition process and stayed involved, first with the purchase and integration of a small Australian firm. By 2009, Faulkner had built his executive team's M&A prowess to the extent that they were able to take on the acquisition of a very large competitor, Hardigg Industries. That nearly doubled revenue. This time, Faulkner brought in a veteran M&A operator he knew from prior work experience to run the integration. Both acquisitions went smoothly.

If you want to make acquisitions, having M&A skills on the management team reduces risk. Yet many midsized firms think they can learn how to do it on the fly. If you want to take that chance, I strongly advise you to keep that first acquisition small and in the same vertical. In addition, if you lack M&A integration expertise, hire experienced people who do. Finally, make sure your best operations executive can focus on the acquisition. Free him from his other duties.

As a CEO, I did my first acquisition in 1999. The company

we bought, Rinehart Fine Arts, produced posters and other decorative art that winds up framed on office and home walls. I made that deal without a lick of M&A experience. Fortunately, Rinehart was a small version of my own fine art publishing business, Bentley Publishing Group. After we closed the deal, we simply packed up their warehouse and shipped their products to our facility. The seller stayed on in a consultative role. I had a veteran M&A coach mentor me. While it was a strain on my team, the integration was orderly. And with each successive acquisition (we did four from 1999 to 2004), my team's experience grew. So did the speed and efficiency of the integrations.

Every acquisition has missteps and surprises. Midsized firms without acquisition experience will have a much more difficult time at this game.

Assessing How Much Integration You Need

The best acquirers don't bite off more than they can chew. They figure out how much integration will be necessary and they back off deals that look likely to overtax their team. Thus, they make the right trade-off between the size of an acquisition (that is, how much additional revenue it will provide) and the complexities of bringing it into the fold (the cost and effort of getting that revenue).

The first determination a good acquirer makes is about the size of the deal, answering the essential question: "How big a deal can we pull off at this time?" Too small an acquisition can be a lot more work and money than it's worth. As a result, many skilled acquirers have a minimum deal size as a part of their screening process. This avoids wasting time on due diligence.

Surprisingly, if the target company is under $5 million in revenue, there is a high likelihood that due diligence will be especially difficult and costly. Small companies frequently have poor reporting and accounting systems. Therefore, the smaller the company, the greater the risk that there will be surprises after closing. Surprises are always bad. And while buying a small business is unlikely to kill you (as the initial cost won't be high), the other costs—time, staff, and distraction—may be painful. Skip them unless there is a compelling reason and no better alternatives exist.

Companies that are a bit bigger—say, more than 20 percent of your size—have the potential to move your needle. But they can be a big challenge, far bigger than their size might indicate. The $25 million revenue firm you acquire could suffer a loss that could eat deeply into your $100 million company's profits. In fact, it could erase those profits altogether.

Now consider buying a firm that is 75 percent of your firm's size. That's a transformational deal. A deal of that size would certainly move your revenue needle. Of course, it could also sink your company if it doesn't work out.

The risk of a major deal comes in five flavors. The first is financial. Larger businesses in trouble consume cash much faster than smaller ones. The second risk is human capital. The higher the head count, the greater the likelihood there will be people problems and the more effort you'll need to expend to keep the staff productive. The third heightened risk is the integration of systems and facilities. Every factory that needs to be closed or IT system that must be migrated rapidly ratchets up your burden. The fourth risk is complexity. When you acquire a large company, it usually has a lot of customers and customer segments. That may mean it has differentiated marketing, sales, and customer service practices for each segment. That's a lot of complexity to swallow. The fifth and final big risk is time. Although all integrations are best done quickly, some *have* to be done quickly, especially those in which you've invested a significant percentage of your company's capital.

You need an expeditious return on that capital to relieve the debt burden you've assumed. And that return depends in large part on getting that integration done quickly so you can begin retrieving the revenues and economies that inspired the acquisition in the first place.

With such large risks, big deals should only be undertaken when a midsized company has a compelling reason to do so, a reason to bet the company. And if you're going to bet the company, you'd better first do in-depth financial modeling that includes worst-case scenarios. What happens if your acquisition's revenue and profitability declines and new products under development bomb? Your operating executives with hands-on experience on how a company such as the one you're looking to buy makes its money must dig into the details. They must factor in factory throughput, inventory turns by SKU, costs of quality assurance, government compliance, and so on. This is not high-level financial work. This is number crunching. But only by embracing the details can you model the scenarios and make a good decision.

The CEO needs to remind his executives that they'll be held accountable for delivering the numbers they provided in the plan. The sales VP will be accountable for exploiting that new market. The COO will be accountable for delivering the cost savings he projected. The business unit GM will be accountable for bottom-line profits in the plan. And maybe the CEO is personally responsible for realizing the strategic value. All this is determined and written before the board reviews or approves the deal. This should eliminate Pollyanna-ish projections based on best-of-all-possible-worlds assumptions.

Buy-in before you buy in. Carve it in stone.

So if you decide your firm has the capability to integrate a company you want to acquire, how will you decide how much integration you need and can accomplish? Should you merge the marketing and sales staffs? The product lines? The IT and HR systems? The offices? More? Less?

Too much integration can overcomplicate an acquisition and break the bonds, processes, and teams that made the company worth acquiring in the first place. Too little can mean you won't be able to eliminate enough duplicative costs to gain value, or the management teams won't gel and benefit from cross-fertilization. A merger should make 1+1 = much more than 2, not less. The best way to do that is to resist integrating processes, systems, product lines, departments, and other items that yield only minor cost savings, especially if they're providing a competitive advantage as they stand. *Big gains from M&A rarely come from small cost savings.* The disruption and friction of integrating even one piece of an acquisition's business into yours can far outweigh the small savings you can achieve.

After you assess how much your firm will need to integrate the products, processes, and strategies of an acquisition, the final element of successful acquisitions is doing that integration smoothly.

Bringing Discipline to Integration

The best time to begin planning for how you will integrate an acquisition's business into your own is before you sign the contract. And the executives you need at the table are not just your corporate development team. You should get the rest of your operating team involved: the product line, marketing, sales, manufacturing, distribution, finance, and other senior managers in your company who will be asked to work with their counterparts at the soon-to-be-acquired company.

My research shows that this is especially important for midsized companies in the $500 million to $1 billion range.

In these companies, the operating team should be helping the corporate development team and the CEO and CFO conduct the due diligence on the acquisition target. If they are to handle the integration, or ever run the business, they need to know what the company is buying long before they're responsible for it. And you need their input on whether the acquisition is advisable before you close the deal. Early involvement by the operating staff allows them to align to the strategic intent of the merger. Once they start operating they may be too encumbered to align to the CEO's vision, and may steer off course.

Barry Karlin, cofounder and former CEO of CRC Health Group, the largest provider of chemical dependency and behavioral health-care treatment services in the United States, agrees. He built his firm through more than thirty acquisitions between its founding in 1995 and when he left in 2010. (In 2006 Bain Capital purchased the company for $723 million.) Today, CRC revenue is in the $450 million range. Karlin told me that the "likelihood of an acquisition's failure goes up the less the operating people are involved during deal making."

Furthermore, if you plan to keep the management team of your target acquisition in place, this can be a great time to get them involved in planning for life after the merger.

This is the best possible way to do an acquisition, but it's not the way it's often done in the real world. In many midsized firms, the CEO (with or without the corporate development department) finds, assesses, and largely buys businesses on her own. Once the deal is done, it's handed over to the operating executives. This approach will greatly increase the risk of failure, as your people will be coming in cold. It will take time for them to learn the lay of the land, build relationships, and assess the acquired company's systems and capabilities—time your business can ill afford, time in which key employees may leave, and time that degrades the return on invested capital.

So getting the right people at the table is important before the close. After the close, you need to integrate your acquisition quickly and with discipline. The place to begin is with a carefully crafted plan, one that articulates the premise of the acquisition and lays out the goals and dates for meeting them. That plan can't sit on a shelf; it must be created and monitored by the managers responsible for implementing it.

Here is where you need to get your crackerjack project management team in the game. (Remember I told you that you needed one in chapter 1, "Letting Time Slip-Slide Away.") For a midsized company, the integration of an acquisition— particularly a big one—will be where your project managers earn their pay.

Whether the integration takes ninety days or ninety weeks, you'll need a governance board to oversee the activities. The deal board should consist of leaders from the buying firm, selling firm, project management function, and corporate development and operating business unit leaders. The board must report to the CEO of the acquiring firm and monitor the progress of the integration.

Not only does this board wire top management into the integration's progress, it provides the seller's management team with a high-level venue to vent. This is a problem in many acquisitions. The seller's top team feels they don't have the ear of anyone at the top of the firm that acquired them. They can't get important decisions made because they can't get the attention of their new bosses. They feel like strangers in a strange land. Anger and plummeting morale are sure to follow.

A deal board will help you short-circuit all that angst. I advise having one in place for at least two years after a deal closes. It should meet monthly (just like a corporate board) and discuss the key indicators of integration progress.

I hope I haven't scared you off completely from making acquisitions. They require lots of work, people who know what they're doing, a rigorous integration plan, and a board that's monitoring its progress. But that's all doable. It's not rocket science. And, when done well, acquiring the right company can turbocharge your growth.

But if you don't do it well, well, it can kill you.

Rollups: Useful for Studying Midsized Acquisitions

One of the best kinds of midsized companies from which to learn about acquisitions is a rollup. A rollup is created by a team that identifies a highly fragmented market served by many companies. The idea of a rollup is that by acquiring many former competitors, a company can create huge economies of scale in purchasing, production, selling, finance, and many other processes, as well as provide more professional marketing and salesmanship to all. To succeed at rollups, the acquirer must perfect its skills at selecting acquisition candidates and then integrating their businesses after the deals are done.

Often funded by private equity, rollups need to grow fast and dramatically to more than recoup the acquisition prices they pay. They must minimize the risk of each acquisition and increase the level of operational efficiency. CRC Health Group, funded by North Castle, Credit Suisse, and finally Bain Capital, discussed in this chapter, is a rollup.

For any acquirer, a study of successful rollups is a study of acquisition best practices. But the lessons rollups provide are particularly important for midsized companies as the rollup's acquisitions are the primary driver for its growth, and because it often puts all or a majority of its capital at risk.

United Site Services (mentioned earlier in this chapter) launched in 2000 when Ken Ansin and his business partner identified the portable restroom industry as ripe for consolidation. They began buying small firms, rolling them up into a company that by 2003 was generating $120 million in revenue and was sold to private equity firm Odyssey Investment Partners at an excellent multiple. Odyssey tripled the business in three years through acquisitions and sold it to DLJ Merchant Banking Partners in June 2006. The company has continued to make acquisitions, eighty-three and counting by 2012.

The first thing Ansin did right was to choose a good market. "In looking at the market, we quickly realized that we could buy businesses for about 1.0 to 1.1 times revenue," says Ansin. "As we talked to different businesses in the industry, we quickly learned that not only could we buy them for what we felt was a pretty reasonable multiple, but most of these businesses were, if you'll excuse the pun, *relieved* to sell. Typically, they were operating on a shoestring. It was Mom in the office and Dad in the field with Uncle Joe. They didn't have a lot of business acumen; they didn't have a lot of computer processes; they didn't have the bonus systems we use to incentivize the drivers, which was a big part of our model."

But United's first acquisition, in January 2000, wasn't a Mom and Pop and Uncle Joe. It was the largest player in the New England market, Handy House, a $15 million firm.

"We lucked out with the first company we bought because it was really *the* player in New England. And so, as we folded in ancillary mom-and-pops around them, the combining was already done for us because the mom-and-pops we folded in were so much smaller than the first company we bought. So it was just natural to use the first company's yard, its trucks, and so on," says Ansin.

United went on to buy six other New England firms in its first year, growing market share and increasing its pricing power. For large-scale public events such as rock concerts, United was soon the only game in town. The company focused on Boston, Springfield, Hartford, and Providence, and then moved south. In this controlled expansion, it developed its method for acquiring, honed its integration skills, and confirmed the hypothesis that it could increase the efficiency of the portable toilet businesses through scale. United's New England operation grew to about $35 million revenue in eighteen months before it looked to the next region.

While making seven acquisitions in eighteen months was hardly slow growth, United's decision to keep its first acquisitions within easy driving distance of its home base was critical as it built its knowledge base and bench strength.

Ansin and his management team learned some key lessons early on. Some acquisitions came with other ancillary businesses, such as rental operations: fences for construction, other equipment, and trailers. But Ansin found the best approach was to keep the business focused, so United ditched the rental businesses and restricted itself to port-a-potties. It also found it needed to send teams of middle managers to new acquisitions to replace the mom-and-pop operators immediately, and then hire and train local management, inculcating the United corporate culture.

"Sometimes, in really important markets, we'd move people out from headquarters that could do a good job of conveying the company story, the company culture. We didn't find any more efficient way than that," Ansin says.

Remote-control acquisitions are high risk. Ansin's commitment to making the investment necessary to send teams on-site to acquired locations was critical to the company's success and is a best practice.

United's next targets were in the Washington, D.C., Raleigh-Durham, and Florida areas. In each region, the first acquisition became the hub, as was the case with Handy House. United would keep the acquired firm's yard and facilities, but implement its own IT system and work processes.

Ansin's team immediately integrated each smaller acquisition adjacent to the hub, moving equipment, contracts, and customers. They kept the local brand names alive just long enough to make customers comfortable with the United Site Services name.

Fast integrations are always best. In this situation, the acquirer knew all it needed to know about the business; there was no new technology or other risks that could upset the selling team. Quick acquisitions reduced costs faster and allowed the traveling integration team to move quickly to the next acquisition.

United drove relentlessly for efficiency. It developed company-wide incentive plans that rewarded high performers. It standardized equipment and processes, selling off old equipment from the acquisitions and replacing it. The company had a deal with Ryder that allowed it to upgrade trucks and equipment almost immediately. It evaluated leases, and bought out many to reduce costs.

United's geographic expansion continued. Starting in mid-2001, the acquisitions came at a pace of four per quarter. They tackled new metro areas one at a time: Atlanta, Dallas/Fort-Worth, and eventually as far west as Las Vegas. The day after a new acquisition deal closed, one or more managers from corporate would arrive. On the first day, they'd figure out who they wanted to keep. Within the first week, a general manager from headquarters would move in, along with an IT guy and a customer service person.

With this approach, the platform acquisitions that would become regional hubs had United processes implemented within the first month. Customer outreach began on day one, and old customers of the acquired companies experienced new levels of attention and service. The smaller companies United rolled up (many under $3 million revenue) were fully integrated within thirty days. "Soon after we started growing in this business, we had the operations piece figured out," Ansin explains. "There wasn't much we didn't understand."

Only toward the end of 2003 did United centralize its accounting function nationwide. Integrating only those processes that add value can decrease integration complexity.

Strategic Acquisition Payoff Grid

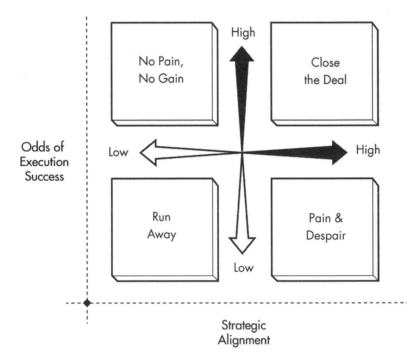

FIGURE 4-1: The upper right quadrant represents high-payoff acquisitions: those that are perfect for your strategy and that you will execute well. The lower left quadrant contains wasteful disasters, since they are a poor strategic fit and you'll fail in execution as well. In the upper left are deals that are easy to absorb, but don't move the needle for the acquirer because they are strategically irrelevant. In the lower right quadrant are potentially great opportunities that will be fumbled by the team over and over again, but efforts to make it work will continue because of the strong strategic alignment, draining resources over time and eroding ROI.

It's important to be careful when making an acquisition, but it's equally important not to shrink from the difficulties. Growing through acquisition can work well for midsized companies. Indeed, as has been the case for United, it can work extremely well.

Figuring out if any given acquisition is right for your company is paramount. After all the research I've done, I've created a detailed online assessment tool for vetting acquisitions at www.ceotoceo.biz/mightytools.html

To boil it all down into a simple concept, having a high payoff to strategic acquisitions means having very high odds of execution success (a good deal and good integration) and buying a firm with excellent strategic alignment. When you are sure you have both, close the deal fast! When you have neither, run away. Run. Say no to deal fever—and yes only to high payoff acquisitions.

5

Operational Meltdown

Can anything ever be wrong with having a growing top line? Can there ever be a problem when you combine that robust top line with a rigorously lean operation?

Actually, yes, there can be. Combining an attempt at rapid growth with a too-skinny operational model can lead to a situation where there's too much work to do and not enough people or other resources to do it well.

When that happens, your business will feel the stress.

There often comes a point in the life of a midsized business when it goes from happily hectic and busy to unhappily overwhelmed and chaotic. That's when the wheels come off the bus. That's when employees start quitting without giving notice; customers begin complaining about poor service; and vendors, tired of waiting to get paid, stop shipping product.

It's not a pretty picture. That's a portrait of an operational meltdown, which happens to be the fifth silent killer of midsized company growth.

When a firm is small, it can usually resolve a rush of orders by hiring a few extra people or buying a new computer server. Remember Instagram? Its founders launched the San Francisco–based social media company on October 6, 2010, and immediately had so much demand (twenty-five thousand users the first day) that it had to work twenty-four hours straight to keep its servers from melting down. So Instagram called in its Stanford

University connections, moved to Amazon servers that night, and within a month was set up to handle a million users.[1] You can do that if you're small, nimble, and technologically adept. (Having Stanford on speed dial helps, too.)

By contrast, big firms typically have well-established operations functions staffed by people who have devoted their lives and careers to making sure the trains run on time.

But both situations are a far cry from what goes on at most midsized firms. Many are not likely to be able to fix big operational meltdowns in one night, ten, or even a hundred. Midsized companies are too big, with too many moving parts.

How Hot Will It Get?

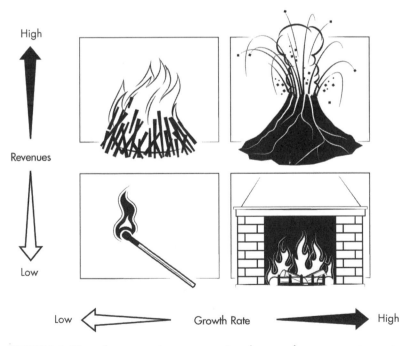

FIGURE 5-1: Very fast-growing companies that are larger are at greatest risk of a damaging operational meltdown.

What's more, their executives can't put their daily responsibilities on hold while they attend to operational glitches, no matter how threatening they may be in the long run.

For midsized firms, the higher the growth rate and the bigger the firm, the hotter the fire. At some point, every business can melt down.

Not even rapidly increasing revenue can bail a midsized company out when critical operations begin to falter. In fact, when this killer is at work, when operations head south, sales growth can prevent an organization from addressing its problems in a timely, effective manner. It can even exacerbate them. Growing revenue is always a good thing. But if that growth goes hand in hand with an operational meltdown, a company will see those top-line gains disappear before they can drop to the bottom line. That's why this killer is so insidious. It often does its work under the cover of success, silently undermining a business's foundations and putting its future growth in jeopardy.

In this chapter we will look at the primary causes of operational meltdown in midsized businesses, and what their leaders can do to avoid them.

Growth + Chaos = Waste

You probably don't believe me. You figure if a business is growing, if sales are increasingly reliably year after year, the business is sound. If money is flowing in, any problem—even an operational meltdown—has to be easy to fix. How could it possibly be a killer? Well, let me tell you the story of a company that grew itself into a nightmarish hole. The company in this story shall remain nameless.

It was launched in 2008 by acquiring a product line from a larger business. The product line's new owners got the larger company's inventory but they had to build their computer systems from scratch. Starting up with $4 million in revenue seemed as if it would be easy, especially as the company was outsourcing manufacturing and fulfillment. However, its industry norm demanded a fairly complicated sales compensation plan, so the IT system that supported that plan was similarly complex.

The new company's CEO was an experienced executive with a flair for marketing and sales. If something was customer facing, he understood it. But he also knew that when it came to operations and especially to IT, he wasn't so strong.

Sales at the new company grew and grew. But that growth, combined with weak operational and IT expertise, led to several operational meltdowns. The wrong products were shipped. There were computer system glitches that generated incorrect billings and charges that required manual fixes eating up thousands of employee hours. But the products were good and the company kept growing. Still, the ownership had to kick in some more capital to sustain it.

The company retained a third-party logistics firm to handle warehousing and distribution. It hired an affordable software outfit to modernize its website and make it more functional. Money was tight; after all, this was still a start-up. The software firm put the company on an experimental platform that failed. The platform's March 2008 launch looked good on the surface, but all the actual automation had failed so the company was forced to hire dozens of office workers (they affectionately referred to themselves as hamsters) who labored behind the scenes to do the work the automation was supposed to do. The firm then hired a VP of IT who fired the software firm and chose another vendor. This vendor did a better job on the basics, but it was quite expensive and never delivered a stable platform or functional administrative interfaces, effectively putting itself in a position where it could hold the company hostage. The start-up company's CEO eventually fired the VP of IT who had chosen the second vendor.

The hamsters hopped from one wheel to the next, mailing out checks to cover shipping charges as the software couldn't automate the process of providing the free shipping its customers had been promised. Finally, as 2010 approached, a minimally viable software system was stabilized...and then the logistics provider crumbled. Some deliveries were very late. Others were sent to the wrong people and contained the wrong stuff. That put the business's reputation at risk.

The CEO hired a VP of logistics with great credentials. But he prided himself on cost reduction. He brought in a low-cost logistics firm, firing the first logistics firm before the new one was ready to start. Knowing that 60 percent of its business was about to walk away, the old logistics provider immediately terminated account management and supervisory staff. Not surprisingly, shipments, already in bad shape, got much worse. The hamsters continued to sweat on their wheels.

By 2011, with sales humming along and the hamsters running as fast as they could, the firm was nearing $50 million in revenues, about twelve times its first-year revenues four years earlier. That's great growth, isn't it? It made for an impressive top line. And the company was determined to protect it and its customers from the consequences of its operational problems. The new, cheaper logistics provider ended up costing the company 50 percent more per shipment than the old one, eating into margin, but at least the orders were going out.

The CEO then dismissed the new VP of logistics. He'd almost destroyed the company in the ill-planned changeover between logistics vendors and wouldn't (or couldn't) grasp a key company value: that business continuity and high service levels trumped low cost and supply chain efficiency.

The cost of the long-running operational meltdown was now in the millions, and that impressive top-line growth was not feeding the bottom line but rather funding the impact of the meltdown. All those sales, all those revenues, and the company was still struggling to provide the experience it had promised its customers.

Predictably, ownership was not happy. The CEO estimated that the company had wasted $13 million between the salaries of the hamsters, the failed IT initiatives, and the costs of keeping customers happy amid the chaos. That money could have been invested elsewhere by the owners or used to grow even faster. And while the company's $50 million in revenues sounded good, it was a drop in the bucket compared to its competitors, some with revenues in the billions. The leadership of the company was so distracted (and worried) by the meltdown that it decided to slow the company's plans for geographic expansion that could accelerate their growth until it could get a handle on operations. But doing that wasn't so easy.

Operations continued to falter. The software platform that had been created only a few years before for a $4 million company (and hadn't been very good then) was woefully inadequate for a $50 million firm that was projected to double its revenues in the coming year. With all the urgent operational problems, plus all the new sales opportunities for a growing sales team, the IT infrastructure was cobbled together with duct tape and chicken wire. Quick patches (hacks) and untested features abounded. The underlying system was slow and many disparate systems were interwoven—without documenting the code, of course. The VP of IT kept everyone happy by delivering features the business requested, but he kept the growing IT infrastructure problem to himself. Naturally, the frequency of system crashes increased. The company poured about $5 million into the black hole IT had become but the problems were intractable. There were no quick fixes.

As a result, the company put its plan to expand internationally on hold. To move into overseas markets, it would need a modernized e-commerce platform, a fully integrated customer relationship management system (CRM), a human resources management (HRM) system, and a new ERP. But the company lacked the IT leadership to climb this mountain and all resources were focused on plugging holes and bailing water. By 2012 the firm crossed the $100 million revenue line and was solidly cash-flow positive. But it seemed no amount of money could give the company the IT systems it needed to succeed internationally, or run efficiently, dependably, and with the tools that would fuel continued growth. Without the right systems, the risk of a catastrophic system failure grew to the point where it would be beyond the capability of a whole cageful of hamsters to disguise. And throwing more and more bodies at something that should be automated was ruinously expensive. The company's CEO brought in a high-level IT consultant who quickly identified the deep-seated IT problems that, unaddressed, would prevent the company from ever expanding its market. The VP of IT was let go, and a new IT leader took his place in mid-2013, about the time the firm crossed the $200 million revenue run rate.

By the end of 2013, the business made a strong commitment to address its technology deficits, attracted needed IT talent, and committed to further investment in its IT infrastructure. And it *finally* made the hard choice to let go of the overspent legacy systems and further invest in the systems it had long needed with a focus on architecture that would allow the business to scale and globalize. The hardest decision for this market-focused company was to delay growth-related programs until the systems could be implemented and tested.

This company had a good product, good cash flow, good salespeople, good everything...except operational competence. Between its founding in 2008 and the end of 2013, it did well, but as meltdown followed meltdown, it left a lot of money and potential growth on the table. In retrospect, doing well prevented it from taking its systemic problems more seriously and addressing them effectively.

Most companies aren't as fortunate as this one. They get a big opportunity (or growth spurt), disappoint their customers by under-delivering due to operational problems, and then shrink back down to a size they can manage. If they're lucky, they may get a second chance. Many do not.

The Four Signs of Operational Meltdown

So, is growth bad? Of course not. Growth is good, especially if you support it with the right teams and systems. But if your operations aren't matched to your growth, your business can turn sour rapidly, even in the midst of plenty. And unlike our start-up, the stories rarely end happily. You'll know you're heading for an operational meltdown if you recognize any of these four telltale signs:

1. *An overbearing sales culture.* A company I know was founded by a salesman. He was passionate and knew how to ring the bell. But as his company grew, he undervalued and underpaid his finance and operational executives. It's not surprising that those managers were weak. Bungled shipments meant customers didn't pay the balances on their invoices in a timely manner. Product had to be reshipped. Inventory grew. Turns slowed. Costs rose. The CEO, frustrated, often asked, "What's so difficult about getting the product out?" Meanwhile, his salespeople (genetically programmed to say yes) kept on saying yes to more and more customers. Eventually, the company started delivering so late that those customers delayed payments by months. The consequent cash shortfall, combined with the deeply embedded problems in the business's culture, ultimately caused the business to go bankrupt even as the salespeople kept ringing the bell.

2. *An outdated IT or physical infrastructure.* Small companies can add infrastructure in little chunks as the business

grows. But the bigger a midsized organization gets, the longer it takes to build facilities and IT, and the more work it takes to teach teams to use them effectively. I hear some operations hotshots boast about "changing the wheels on the car while it's moving," but this is a last-resort way to do anything. Really. Would you try to change the wheels on your car while it's moving? I don't think so. Yes, building infrastructure takes resources away from new product development and customer services, and you don't like doing that. And when things are running well, it's easy to ignore infrastructure needs in favor of growing the top line. But what use is growing the top line if your infrastructure keeps draining the bottom line and putting your company at risk of a meltdown? Pretty soon, your top-line growth will stall. If you try to build a new infrastructure as you drain your resources trying to grow, you'll get run over.

3. *A skills shortage.* Sadly, many high-growth companies outgrow their teams. That may not be the fault of employees swamped by the day to day. Operations is a *profession*. And even if you have those professionals, midsized businesses need them to interact with all the business's functions. Team play is an art in itself. You'll know you're about to hit the wall when you have important initiatives and challenges and no one competent, available, or willing to lead them.

4. *Too many eggs, not enough baskets.* One of the reasons some CEOs hesitate to spend on infrastructure is that they are overly dependent on one or two big customers and see the diversion of resources to operations as a risk. Committing to fixed expenses and a big cash spend is very scary when your sales are too concentrated. Of course, having an operational meltdown is also a good way to lose that big, key customer. And just as big customers bring big jumps in scale and complexity, so too do acquisitions. One day the firm is

$40 million and the next it's $80 million. Not only does that increase in size bring its own challenges, but there is extra work to do to integrate the two firms. (See chapter 4, "Fumbled Strategic Acquisitions," page 95.)

Rollups, where a company buys a number of related firms, are especially vulnerable to operational meltdown. JetDirect Aviation, an air charter company based in Weymouth, Massachusetts, rapidly built a $500 million business by acquiring a dozen charter businesses. It let four years fly by without really trying to integrate them, focusing instead on dominating the market through more acquisitions and addressing financial issues by raising investment capital. By the time it tried to centralize the accounting function, the people who owned the client relationships (crucial in the charter business) had been sent packing. On top of that, the integration was done poorly. Angry clients refused to pay the incorrect bills the faulty system generated, and the people who they trusted to take care of their planes and interests were gone. Cash vanished. Within five years of its first acquisition, the company filed for bankruptcy.

So you want to grow, but you want to do so in a sustainable way, and you want your business to be able to support future growth. Like it or not, that means you have to invest in the infrastructure and processes that will reduce the risk of suffering an operational meltdown.

Feeling nervous that your company might be vulnerable to an operational meltdown? Take this online assessment (www. ceotoceo.biz/mightytools.html) to employ the kind of discovery I use with high-growth clients.

How to Raise your Company's Melting Point

Midsized companies must take two fundamental steps to reduce their risk of operational meltdown. First, leadership

What Is Your Company's Melting Point?

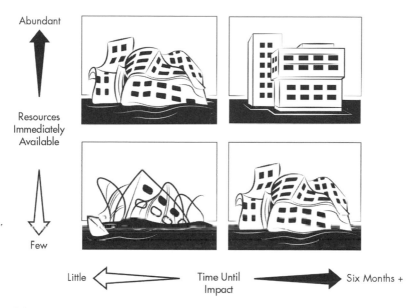

FIGURE 5-2: Increasing operational resilience is like increasing your company's melting point. How effective you'll be is a by-product of the time you have until the projected operational meltdown and the resources (money and talent) you can throw at the problem immediately.

must inculcate an organizational mind-set that insists upon the consistent and dependable delivery of products or services. This mind-set must be buttressed by operational resilience. The business has to be prepared for problems and surprises, and it must have the wherewithal to bounce back. This will raise your company's melting point, taking it from lead (which melts at 327°F) toward tungsten (which melts at 6,150°F).

This is crazy talk for many young companies relentlessly focused on finding customers and coming up with new ideas. And, in truth, they probably shouldn't spend too much money on operations because they need every nickel and minute they have to survive. CEOs who have led early-stage companies struggle to shift their focus to operations as their businesses become midsized. Life gets less exciting. There is less of that exhilarating high-risk, high-reward, high-adrenaline feel.

Second, midsized companies must get serious about investing in future operations. Bigger companies need bigger systems and more expensive executives (and more of them). Entire companies have been launched for less money than it costs a midsized company to upgrade an ERP system or move headquarters to a bigger building. Early-stage entrepreneurs and small-business owners struggle to understand (and justify) what it takes to support the operations of a midsized firm.

It's an unavoidable fact of life that many CEOs who have the mojo to create new companies from scratch don't have the same enthusiasm for day-to-day operations. They'll do their best, and may try to discipline themselves to love operations the way they love new ideas, new customers, big orders, and new technologies. However, many of them will fail at becoming operationally focused.

If that's you, you'll need to bring in an executive who loves operations, heart and soul, and hates risk and sloppiness. This executive (perhaps titled chief operating officer, or "COO") will never become CEO. Don't ask the COO to get in front of prospective customers, as their focus will be to minimize complexity, not to say yes to special requests. It will also be to design and deploy systems, measures, and processes that will keep an unblinking eye over the business's everyday activities, shipment after shipment. The COO will do whatever has to be done to satisfy customers and deliver on your promises.

The first operations executive you hire should report to you. He will require your full support, as the COO will be the tip of the spear that will shift your firm's culture from risk taking toward risk avoiding. The COO will be a security blanket for many executives in your organization who live in fear of yet another operational disaster—a shipping delay, a prolonged stock-out, a systems crash, a factory shutdown, a compliance issue, a lawsuit, a recall, or any of the other horrors that are born of operational meltdown.

Supporting this executive may mean reducing your company's speed to market. Operations work may eat up capital that you would prefer to spend on new features or products. Your salespeople's promises to customers may be constrained as the COO insists that all promises be kept. You may even lose some sales. In other words, supporting this executive may reverse many of the practices that made you successful as a smaller, younger business.

This change will be hard for everyone. But midsized firms that deliver on their promises can turn into big businesses. Solid midsized firms can be trusted by mega-firms to deliver, and deliver as promised; small firms can't. So while supporting an operations exec can have downsides, they are far outweighed by the upside.

Take Pride in Operational Excellence

Most young or smaller firms that survive take great pride in making a sale. The rest is anticlimactic: shipping the goods or delivering the service. But a midsized firm must also have a sense of pride in operational excellence. In my own company, we took pride in working for days to prepare a large shipment, and then in seeing the trailer, perfectly packed, drive off on time. Getting the sale was a victory; shipping the order was another. We celebrated both.

Tear a page out of the sales leadership book and develop this sense of pride within your organization by following these three steps:

1. **Set clear targets** for operations; assess the risks to achieving them, and share those risks with the leadership team.

2. **Deploy and track operational success metrics** in the same way you set and track sales goals. Those measures of success should be visible to the entire leadership team.

3. **Celebrate operational milestones** across the company (just like a big sale) with recognition and rewards. When your sales team achieves a big win, do you throw a party? Do you hand out bonuses? Of course. Do the same for on-time delivery.

Too often the people on the operations team only get noticed when something goes wrong. The blame is usually placed on the people, not on a lack of resources or unreasonable organizational expectations. And when things do go well, all too often the leadership concludes everything is hunky-dory and nothing needs to be done to ensure future success. This sort of benign neglect usually leads to a chronically under-resourced operations function that will be vulnerable to regular meltdowns that will ruin the firm's reputation and kill its prospects for growth.

Another cultural shift a company must make as it grows from small to midsized is from a short-term focus on immediate results to a longer-term commitment to stability. For example, one cloud software provider would throw together some undocumented, barely tested code to test-market a new offering. This saved money on ideas that failed to garner enough demand. However, those that succeeded were not rebuilt to be efficient or robust. Nor was the code ever documented. (That would take too long.) Instead, resources were allocated to new products to grow the top line. Ultimately, the cost of maintaining so many poorly written software offerings began to pile up. Support costs soared. Then a security breach damaged the firm's reputation and its growth came to a screeching halt.

Almost by definition, a midsized firm has proven that it can survive. But to thrive, it must make the shift to lowering its ongoing cost of operations (which often requires investing in equipment or processes or both) as well as taking precautions against the surprises and shocks that will inevitably come as years of operations roll by.

Invest in Operations

If you've raised the profile of operations within your organization to the point where it is as important as sales, the question arises, "Well, what's the proper level of investment?" An experienced and competent operations executive will only ask for what is needed, understanding that taking money away from sales and marketing will lead to layoffs and the underutilization of operational infrastructure.

The answer to the correct level of operational investment lies in scenario planning. At the scale at which most midsized firms run, this is a detailed exercise that studies the capacity of each step in the operational process. The scenarios created cannot be static. They begin with current production levels, and then take into account projected increases in volume and the length of time it should take operations to scale up.

For each level of activity, top management must identify the critical path and time frames for investment. Some operations can be stood up (made ready to operate) within a month. Others, a production bakery, for example, can take six to ten months. Once the management team understands these time frames, they must then forecast the financial impact of each scenario, clarifying the financial risks and capital requirements.

For example, one firm, relying on Asian-based suppliers, was failing to develop the new, innovative products it felt it needed to grow. The firm assessed corrective options ranging from hiring a third-party U.S.-based development firm to opening and staffing a product development office in China. In the end, they chose a middle path, hiring a highly skilled U.S. engineering leader and moving him to China for six months, accelerating the first new batch of products with stateside support. After their first product debuted, they decided to assess the next steps. This was a prudent, thoughtful, financially responsible process that mitigated risks while achieving the desired ends.

Grow with a Plan

Most businesses at risk of operational meltdown aren't those that are growing steadily at 10 percent or even 20 percent per year. Businesses risk meltdown when growth is high and the company needs to have a significantly different type of operation than it had the year before. This happens when, for example, one person handling sourcing and fulfillment suddenly becomes a ten-person operations department. It happens when a company is selling domestically one year and the next it is shipping product on four continents. When these things happen, fixed costs start looking like variable costs. New buildings, systems, and other large, long-term capital assets are purchased regularly.

These high-growth firms are going through a metamorphosis and planning for that scale of change takes hundreds of hours, years of experience, and skill. It is very hard. Most midsized companies (and their leaders) have not gone through it. CEOs (and their partners in the effort, CFOs) who don't embrace the rigor of operational planning and assume that their functional leaders have everything under control are risking an operational meltdown. While the CEO and CFO may not have experience in each of the organization's functional disciplines, they must challenge each leader and examine the processes and assumptions supporting each facet of the operations plan.

The CEO and CFO must examine, assess, and validate six

areas to see if the business can grow sustainably without running the risk of an operational meltdown.

1. **IT and business intelligence.** When companies grow quickly, the demands on IT increase proportionally. This includes databases and subsystems like warehouse management, human capital management, point of sale, customer relationship management, software to handle international business, file-sharing systems, planning and goal-setting systems, and more. And all these systems need to be able to share information in an efficient, seamless fashion. Furthermore, a fast-growing business needs to make quick decisions underpinned by new reports and new metrics. That means investing in business intelligence. Having the capability to produce those reports is critical, as is the ability to analyze the increasing volume of data that feeds them. There are few things that are more frustrating than knowing you have the data that can inform a decision but you're not able to get at it because it's locked in a legacy database that can't talk to your shiny new analytic tools. That's when you have to turn to (and pay) a small army of Excel spreadsheet jockeys to do the work by hand.

2. **Supply chain and vendor relationships.** The venture capital community loves to see its start-ups rely on the infrastructure of others, through outsourcing. That can work well at small scale. But as a company grows to midsize, it must come to grips with the fact that it will be held accountable for the failings of its vendors. Your vendors can (and do) have their own operational meltdowns. They can become distracted. The quality of their service can diminish or fail entirely. Sound operational planning means digging into each of your vendors, verifying their ability and willingness to support your growth, and vetting their plans to minimize their own operational risks.

3. **Talent development and acquisition.** This may sound like a Chinese proverb, but it's true: may your high-growth periods come during down economic cycles. That's when a highly trained workforce is readily available at reasonable salaries. Of course, you can't count on that. The inability to find, develop, retain, and effectively bring talent on board during periods of high growth is one of the biggest triggers of operational meltdown. Companies that are serious about successfully managing high-growth periods must build a tight process—a machine—around employee development, recruitment, and onboarding. (See chapter 7, "Tolerating Dysfunctional Leaders," and the section on onboarding.)

Leaving too many of these tasks—especially training—to the operating team will slow them down. At some point, as you add more staff more quickly, all your operating team's bandwidth will be absorbed in training new employees. In practice, the operating team usually ignores the new hires, leaving them to fend for themselves as it rushes around doing its own job. That's a worst practice. Even the most talented new hires can fail without good onboarding. While the operational managers must be involved in creating the job description, delineating best practices, and making the final choice, HR should handle the training and minimize operational distraction. A good training group can develop tools that will expedite basic training, again leveraging the time of the operating team.

4. **Middle management leadership acumen.** Especially critical for larger midsized companies (about $300 million revenues and up) is that the executives who report to the C-suite be great leaders themselves, and not simply managers. With increasing complexity and growth, the entire C-suite will run out of time and bandwidth to be the only leaders in the firm. This is the same problem that most CEOs have when they transition from a small business to a midsized one, but

it repeats for the entire top team at the next level. Some in the C-suite may not realize the need, or have the competence, to become a leader of leaders. Dictatorial or micromanaging C-suite leaders tend to collect managers who prefer to follow orders rather than lead. Too much of this may mean that in a larger midsized company, fifteen to forty middle managers may have to be replaced, an enormous and daunting task. More on repairing or replacing leaders in chapter 7, "Tolerating Dysfunctional Leaders."

5. **Facilities.** Whether we're talking about offices or factories or warehouses, buildings take time to improve, are hard to change, and absorb large chunks of capital. You need to think long and hard about your facilities investments. Why? Buildings affect people emotionally (you may not care if your office has a window; others may), affecting performance in a bigger way than you might expect. And the quality and geography of your facilities can affect your ability to attract the talent you need. Most midsized companies should retain experts in this area, even if they're expensive. Make your plans early, and then kick them off at the last possible moment to conserve capital. But don't do your planning after the kickoff; that almost guarantees that you'll make a mess of it.

6. **Oversight and compliance.** As small businesses become midsized, they are held to a higher compliance standard. They must strengthen their processes and controls, and the need for oversight becomes acute. A bigger business almost always assumes a greater burden in compliance and often regulation (depending upon its industry). Midsized businesses attract more attention than smaller businesses, from the public, customers, and the government, and are expected to be more diligent about compliance. The cost (in both money and reputation) of being cited as a rule breaker is high.

Preventing Meltdowns: The Art of Budgeting

In early-growth firms, most of the budget flows to customer-facing initiatives. Everything is about getting the next sale. As the sales team brings work in and operations become critical, the work of budgeting becomes more complex. The business's focus expands beyond the next sale to making sure the last one is properly fulfilled. That means execution. That means operations. However, sales and marketing cannot be forgotten, and they need to be funded properly among all the competing demands of the business.

See. It's getting complicated.

In slowly growing companies, the prior year's performance is a great reference point for budgeting. Management can examine and reflect upon last year's inflows and outflows, and make incremental adjustments. However, fast-growing companies do not have that luxury.

To make sure the business can handle its current growth without melting down while preparing for its future growth, the executive team must ask itself the following fundamental questions:

- Is the tension between the performance we're asking of each function and the budget we give them equivalent, or are we (rationally or irrationally) favoring one department or function above all others? And if funds are scarce (which is the norm), are they equally scarce for each function, and for each department within each function, or is one area feasting while others starve?
- How accurate has each functional leader been in forecasting his department's needs? Can we trust these projections?
- If we cannot approve all budget requests (and we probably can't), what can we say no to that would have the least impact on the most important company goals?

For high-growth companies looking to avoid operational meltdowns, an annual budgeting cycle just won't do. Conditions change so fast in times of high growth that budgets must be adjusted and checked either quarterly or every six months. In a quarterly cycle with a calendar year end, the annual budget (if developed in Q4) will be an in-depth review and extension of the Q3 budget update. Toward the end of Q1, each functional leader (in concert with the CFO) should update the budget and add next year's Q1. This makes for a rolling quarterly budget that always covers four quarters forward.

The advantage of budgeting by quarters in high-growth situations is that it enables executives to use their most recent experiences to predict what they'll need for the next two quarters. Doing it year-over-year is both less precise and less tangible, and it allows for fudging and wishful thinking.

This is a fact of business life. You know it. I know it. You may even have done it yourself. Asked to make budget estimates, many executives will ask for more resources than they really need to reduce their risk of underperforming. They'll also ask for more so they can cut their budget if they're asked to without really being forced to get by with less than they think they need to deliver their numbers. Some executives will pad their budget more than others. Some executives will under-promise on results; others are more realistic.

Upon seeing the first version of the budget, the CEO should wonder if the revenue projections are conservative (understated) and the expenses padded (overstated). Combining understated revenue projections with overstated expense projections produces budgets that virtually eliminate profit. The process of getting everyone to the middle point—where the projected revenues are most likely to be achieved, and the expenses and capital expenditures are most likely to be required—is very difficult.

Accordingly, there must be budget oversight, often by the

CEO, certainly by the CFO. This oversight will be exercised in many meetings, some one-on-one with executives, others in teams, where the underlying revenue and expense assumptions—month by month or quarter by quarter—are discussed and vetted. Large cross-functional initiatives should be reviewed and approved by all the functions involved, with one executive responsible for both the budget and the process.

The CFO's role must be much greater than building and wielding the forecasting model. In the end, the CFO must weigh in on whether the budget seems achievable. I advise CEOs and boards to listen to their CFOs! But even though they don't always heed the advice, at least the CFO will have allowed them to make decisions with their eyes wide open, and the CFO will have taken responsibility for having looked under the hood of any budget process.

Part of that review must determine if the organization can actually spend on plan. Many high-growth companies fail to spend budgeted money. They can't execute the plan fast enough, or hire fast enough. They fall behind. They start capital projects too late or can't keep them on schedule. This is bad. Not spending money that's been budgeted to mitigate the risk of operational meltdown often means not being prepared to handle the next wave of growth, and that *will* lead to a meltdown.

The key is to be specific about what tasks need to be done in what period, then to look at who will be responsible for them and how much other work is already on their plates. The workload at companies juggling many projects is best understood when the work is broken down into bite-sized chunks, laid out on a calendar, and reviewed well in advance. (See chapter 1, "Letting Time Slip-Slide Away," for more on project management.)

As a CEO for many years, I've personally grappled with

the dilemma of choosing when to divert budget from sales to operations. Do it too soon, sales may slump. Do it too late, operations may suffer. The key is to wait until your products or services have been proven in the marketplace, and when your sales strategy to grow the top line has been tested and proven effective. Only then (and not sooner) should the company make big operations investments targeting expected growth two or three years out.

A Budget That Said No to Meltdown

Dave's Killer Bread, based in Milwaukie, Oregon, avoided a meltdown despite an overwhelming, unexpected surge in demand for its products. The company was launched in late 2005 as a spin-off from the family bakery NatureBake. It began with revenues of $3 million. Whether it was the story behind the bread (Dave Dahl was an ex-con who returned to the family bakery after doing his time) or its inherent excellence, demand exploded. By summer 2006, the company had maxed out capacity in its 15,000-square-foot bakery.

The company considered outsourcing to grow but rejected that strategy. Making Dave's bread required certified organic bakeries. It chose to turn down new orders rather than risk working with an outsourcing partner it couldn't trust. What Dave's needed was a new facility, but it didn't have the capital.

The company could have gotten that capital by saying yes to several major national retailers that were lining up to sell its bread. But it said no again because it had done the math and knew its budget didn't provide for the investments that would allow it to honor those commitments. Too many firms in Dave's position might have said yes, figuring that they would have months to figure out how to make it work. They might have taken the money, built a new facility, and found out later that the market had evaporated or they didn't have the skills to run a larger operation.

Turning down Costco was particularly hard for Dave's, but Costco understood. Dave's had built a careful budget and forecast, measuring the risk of building a new facility. They could take a small risk for a small facility or a bet-the-farm risk on a huge one. In the end, Dave's took a substantial but, budget in hand, measured gamble.

After initially struggling to get financing, Dave's began planning for a new facility in late 2006 and borrowed $2.1 million to build a new 50,000-square-foot bakery capable of producing 3,000 loaves per hour. They built the bakery in just four months, beginning production there in April 2008. Glenn Dahl, then the CEO, acted as general contractor to expedite the process.

After the new bakery went operational, Costco became a customer, as did many other large national retailers. "I wish we could have expanded sooner, but I don't see how we could have done it," Glenn Dahl says now. "We were always a little behind. We grew fast from $3 million in 2005, and we were always behind the curve on the preparations necessary to keep up with demand."

Saying no preserved the company's reputation with big customers and prospects. Calibrating its growth to its ability to deliver preserved the company's credibility. When it said yes, its customers trusted that it was ready, and by 2011 it was a $50 million business.

That trust was worth even more than that. In March 2013, Dave's sold 50 percent of the company to a private equity firm at a very good multiple to help capitalize an ongoing national rollout. And so the story of Dave's Killer Bread continues. It continues because it said no to growth it wasn't prepared to handle. It said no to outsourcing because it took pride in its product, and it said no to new customers because it took pride in its ability to deliver on its promises. It even said no (at first) to a new facility because its forecast and its budget told it that it wasn't ready...yet.

Dave's story continues today because it avoided an operational meltdown.

6

The Liquidity Crash

Who can forget Liza Minnelli and Joel Grey in the 1972 musical film *Cabaret* singing that "Money makes the world go 'round"? Money also makes business go 'round, but when it runs out, we feel the jolt as operations screech to a halt. Embarrassing and cataclysmic, running out of money—a liquidity crash—utterly consumes the business's attention.

Everything has to wait until the money problem is solved. Indeed, distraction may be the most devastating consequence of running out of money: it keeps everyone, especially the CEO, from attending to the business's business. And that's not good.

The liquidity crash is the sixth silent killer of midsized company growth.

This chapter will take you through some of the root causes of illiquidity; offer descriptions of how good companies managed to survive and sometimes even thrive in the face of a cash crisis; and suggest ways to deal with and (if possible) avoid corporate death in a liquidity crash.

I know. Running out of money seems like an obvious problem, so obvious it hardly bears mentioning. But if it's so obvious, why have so many midsized companies (including my own) come up against it?

Some solid, steady midsized companies run out of money through reckless attempts at growth. I've already covered that in chapter 3 as a silent growth killer in its own right. The other two ways I've seen this silent growth killer take root and run businesses dry are:

1. **Financial erosion.** *A company runs up losses year after year. Eventually and predictably, its cash runs out, the bank pulls out, and the business is in the midst of a full-blown liquidity crash.*

In November 2008, the local board of a national philanthropic organization accepted the resignation of its region's CEO. It had lost $4 million over the previous four years, leaving its line of credit maxed out at $4.2 million and its bank ready to bolt. The new CEO immediately faced meeting a $375,000 payroll with only $40,000 in the bank. Under his predecessor, there was no understanding of the cost of goods sold, no accounting for the expenses required to attract the donations upon which the organization depended. There had been no profit center accounting, and the new CEO quickly discovered that several putative profit centers were, in fact, loss centers. In other words, the nonprofit had no cash management. On top of that, the organization's retail stores were dirty, the staff churned constantly, and inventory was piling up.

Without cash, how could this charitable organization help others if it couldn't help itself?

2. **Shocks to the system.** *A company runs up against something unexpected: a disaster, a lawsuit, the loss of a critical customer, an economic downturn. Cash flow slows and then stops.*

MBH Architects, a leading Northern California architecture firm best known for its design work for retail stores, had consistent growth and profits since its founding in 1989. It had had a banner year in 2007 ($26 million revenues) and a staff of 205. To accommodate its growing business, the firm moved its headquarters and borrowed $3 million to make tenant improvements. Then the great downturn slammed the firm in 2008, and by the end of 2009 revenues had dropped 83 percent. The company had to lay off 74 percent of its staff. The bank froze MBH's line of credit in December 2008, tying management's hands and forcing a million dollar capital call. It couldn't pay the rent on its new headquarters; key clients stopped all work.

The downturn was hardly MBH's fault. But it was in a sector—construction—that was among the hardest hit by the Great Recession. Retailers were not investing in new construction, and MBH was like a runaway Mack Truck barreling down a mountain road, looking for a runaway truck lane to slow it down, yet still walk away alive.

Midsized companies in horrible financial shape—like the two above—can survive for a long time without collapsing. If you're running a company that's starved for cash, don't give up too soon. You can recover. But doing so takes massive amounts of the CEO's time, energy, and faith. And that can distract her from running the business the way it ought to be run. For example, when I ran an art publishing company, there were times when I didn't think I would make payroll. From the time I knew I was in trouble until the payroll was met, all I did was work on finding the money to pay my people. I neglected my customers. And when a customer's order couldn't ship because a key vendor had gone unpaid for too long, then all my time and energy were focused on finding the money to pay them. I was totally focused on getting money; I was completely distracted from everything else.

This is a terrible position. Worse still, being in desperate need of cash makes it harder to get cash. Lenders and investors sense desperation and reasonably worry about a company's viability. Running out of money also reflects badly on the quality of the leadership that has allowed the company to fall into such desperate straits. If you've ever been in a serious cash crunch, you know exactly what I mean.

This is no different for investor-backed firms that have spent too fast, burning through past rounds of funding. The CEOs of those firms spend most of their time making pitch after pitch to investors. They are always hunting for money. What they are not doing is developing their product, planning for the future, working on marketing, or managing their team. And even more than the simple lack of funds, the lack of focus on achieving key milestones is a story that generally ends badly.

If you have a lot riding on your company's success and want to know how well you could survive a liquidity crisis, take this online assessment at www.ceotoceo.biz/mightytools.html. Consider it an extension of this book.

The Ways of Fiscal Prudence

For companies that typically generate profits and are cash-flow positive, the key to avoiding a liquidity crash is to keep enough cash in the kitty during the good times to buy time to fix problems in the bad. This means forever keeping your foot hovering over the spending brake pedal. Strong financial controls (and listening to cautionary counsel) will establish triggers that push the firm to act incrementally, slowing the cash drain or reversing it at an early stage. This helps the company avoid taking such drastic actions as mass layoffs or pulling the plug on strategically important initiatives.

When liquidity ratios are excellent and thickening, companies have lots of latitude. But at some trigger point, fiscal discipline dictates that the most risky, cash-draining activities must cease. Unfortunately, too many companies miss their triggers. They hope that things will work out and that their big break is just around the corner. Wishing and hoping, they breach the second trigger point and then the third. Usually, running out of money is the fifth or sixth trigger, and by that time the company's options have become very, very narrow and what's just around the corner is a liquidity crash.

Hope is not a strategy. Building sound financial controls is.

Make Your Balance Sheet Your Fortress

Think of your balance sheet as a series of crash barriers. If your firm encounters problems with a strong balance sheet, it can decelerate the cash drain by first crashing into short-term bank debt. Then, if needed, it can dip into payables. Then it can slim inventory and receivables, then use some cash reserves, and so on. But as the business breaks through each crash barrier, your velocity had better be slowing because once they're breached they're gone and can't be used again.

The 2008 downturn was a massive test of nearly all companies' crash barriers. Many had what appeared to be low-risk, defensive positions. Yet when sales dropped, say, 40 percent overnight, and banks became highly conservative with credit, cash balance alarms sounded one after another in an incredibly short period of time. A scary ride, to be sure.

Some companies are able to use those balance-sheet barriers to survive the impact of the liquidity crash. But, again, once they've been used, they're gone. So it's critical to rebuild them as soon as you can. That means running the business in a careful, conservative fashion until it generates enough positive cash flow to rebuild the fortress that your balance sheet should be. I've found that running a company at such times is not a lot of fun. I couldn't be creative or reach for big wins (which entail big risks). But...that's life when in the recovery room after a liquidity crash.

Have You Built Enough Crash Barriers to Survive a Liquidity Crash?

FIGURE 6-1: This is the moment you'll need strong crash barriers in your balance sheet to be able to walk away from the crash alive. If the crash barriers aren't there, your company will reach the end of its road.

Mind Your Cash Flow

In the long run, the only reliable way to avoid a cash crisis is to make money, not lose it. Yet many businesses are too tolerant of losses and/or negative cash flow. They scramble trying to find investors and money to borrow. That might work for a while, but not for long. Businesses that fail to make money . . . fail.

I know that sounds simple. That's because it is.

We run businesses for one reason: to supply their owners

with cash flow. While there may be periods of investment, successful CEOs insist on positive results each and every quarter. They don't hope for profits; they demand them. And they take aggressive action when targets aren't met, cutting costs or driving sales higher, if possible. They set targets for profitability, and they react long before the cash account runs low.

And when it does, they cut quickly but they cut strategically.

Cut Thoughtfully

For years, MBH Architects monitored a metric for the utilization of its resources, the number of hours billed to clients compared with the total number of available billable resources. During the dramatic downturn that lasted from 2008 through 2010, CEO Dennis Heath and his cofounder John McNulty made staff cuts early and often, managing that utilization ratio carefully.

As soon as the ratio dropped, Heath moved fast. He began layoffs. He stopped bonuses. In August 2008, he and his partners took a 50 percent pay cut and reduced the staff's pay 15 percent to 20 percent. The founders dipped into their own savings. They closed branch offices early, and slashed expenses and nonbillable salaries to keep fixed expenses down. The owners and staff did the janitorial work. They closed an entire floor of their office to save on utility bills.

Still, it wasn't enough. On Tuesday, December 16, 2008, the bank froze MBH's credit line, leaving the company short for that Friday's payroll. On that same day, their largest client, a top-tier retailer with whom MBH had worked for sixteen years, froze all work. They were in trouble, too. MBH could not carry the 113 people it still had on its payroll.

That month, Heath and McNulty decided that they would postpone layoffs until after the New Year, sparing the team bad news over the holidays. McNulty, Heath, their partners, and the controller, Oli Mellows, met over the holiday to prepare for the layoffs.

"We put everybody's name on a three-by-five card, and we went in the conference room," Heath recalls. "We pinned up every card and asked, 'Okay, who do we need? Who do we want to rebuild the firm with?' We needed the best fifty people. Even in a worst-case scenario, we had a few projects that looked like they were steady. We could handle fifty people on that basis and break even for monthly expenses."

The best way to pay your bills in a liquidity crash, such as the one MBH was confronting, is to avoid creating them in the first place. For a professional services firm, the biggest cost is payroll. As MBH's workload fell, its thoughtful approach to staff reduction turned out to be critical to its recovery. The company's focus was on the future. It kept the people it would need to rebuild the firm, not necessarily those that had been loyal in times past. This is really hard to do for most leaders, but it is their duty. Leaders take us into the future.

Reacting quickly to a slump in business is incredibly important. Things can always get worse, and too many firms hope to sell themselves out of harm's way. Profit is like oxygen for a business, and the discipline to cut back quickly is invaluable lest the business asphyxiate. The 2008 downturn was unusually harsh, and for the construction industry particularly so. This was caused not by any failing of MBH's, but by the economy. There was no short-term corrective action that MBH could have taken to stop the revenue decline, although they certainly tried.

One of the most debilitating aspects of a liquidity crash— or any of the growth killers discussed in this book—is that it diverts management's focus from growing and running the business. While the leadership attends to the company's immediate cash problem, the fundamentals of the business can go awry.

Therefore, restricting the management of the crash to a few leaders is a best practice. It leaves the rest of the team free to run the business, and spares them emotional trauma as well. Nonetheless, the whole team must know what's going on, and therefore communications must be planned and regular. At the same time, management must keep morale up, balancing what employees need to know with the reality of what their future might look like so they can make appropriate personal decisions.

By late 2010, MBH's revenues were on the rise. By 2012 its revenues were 84 percent of 2007's peak. The head count stood at 177 and profits actually exceeded 2007's level.

The work MBH did to survive was hard, but it was work well done.

Why We Keep Score

Having executives who have been through fiscal crises can be a big advantage in a liquidity crash. They'll know from hard-won experience where the pressure points will emerge, and they'll understand what deserves the most attention. Feeling confident of a positive outcome is a vital precursor to success with investors, partners, and employees. The performance of the company in the four to six months before a financing round is a key metric for investors, so execution under pressure is crucial. Should the funding not materialize, or if it arrives months late, the ability to cut spending but stay on track is another must-have skill.

A Not-for-Profit's Turnaround

To their credit, the board of the nonprofit company that I mentioned earlier in this chapter found a CEO in 2008 who understood the importance of cash and keeping track of it. The organization had $4 million in losses and a maxed-out credit line, and the new CEO immediately faced making a $375,000 payroll with only $40,000 in the bank. Payroll check float (the time between issuance of the check and the bank processing date) saved the organization for a few weeks, and the CEO instituted daily cash reporting. He rallied his teams to do a full store cleanup before Thanksgiving and, for the first time in years, the company turned a profit that December. January, normally a big loss month, was profitable and cash positive.

The CEO set a $60,000 profit goal for all of 2009, and began encouraging his management team to lead. (They had been sidelined by his micromanaging predecessor.) He also created a written business plan with his team. "I knew we were going to do better than a surplus of $60,000, but I didn't want to tell them," he says. "The team began to make decisions on its own. As we got those small wins, they turned into bigger wins. People started to gain confidence."

The organization closed 2009 with a $1.1 million surplus. Looking for further gains, the CEO knew the organization's culture was still subpar, and he brought in a consultant to help create a high-performance environment. He continued to bake metrics into the business, even implementing a point-of-sale bar code system that allowed for more accurate pricing. He decided on a $2 per item average price increase. That dropped $2 million a year to the bottom line.

Surpluses have steadily increased, and in 2012 the organization recorded a $3.6 million surplus after investing $5 million in capital assets and expanding services. Its bank borrowings have dropped to $2 million, while it carries a $4 million average cash balance. Its balance sheet had become a fortress. With half of 2013 booked, surpluses are higher than they were in 2012.

Bookkeeping 101

Too many firms simply don't go a good job of keeping score. (The not-for-profit didn't, and look what that got it.) Their accounting processes don't collect general ledger information in useful ways.

This is dangerous. If you don't know where your money is coming from and if you don't know where it's going, how can you decide in a crash crunch how, where, or whether to cut or invest? You can't. Putting transactions in the right place is the foundation of all business decision making. Lenders and investors must have confidence in your books before they'll give you money. Keeping clear of a liquidity crash requires that you know enough to detect it as it brews so you can manage it. Fix your accounting processes without delay. If you don't, the following situation could happen to you.

A growing financial services firm hired a new CFO in 2004. It was proud to show him financial statements reporting that revenues had doubled to $200 million and profits were $20 million. Yet somehow the firm was running short of cash. After three months of pre-audit work and investigation, the CFO adjusted the books to reflect GAAP for revenue recognition issues and material errors. It became clear that, while cash revenues were indeed $200 million for the year, the correct GAAP net revenues were actually $30 million and profits were $2 million. Surprise!

After delivering a painful restatement to lenders and investors, and also creating and presenting a new and detailed monthly and three-year forecasting model validated by historical data, the firm was able to refinance its $25 million bank debt with a new lender. That fueled continued growth. A few months later, a great acquisition opportunity surfaced and the firm was able to increase its loan facility to $75 million to close the deal. Solid budgeting and forecasting gave both management and lenders clear visibility and confidence that the firm could grow and thrive. Four years later, it hit $400 million in (real) revenues with excellent profitability.

Midsized firms often need short-term help to clean up their books so they can make good financial decisions. Some financial services firms such as Robert Half, ManpowerGroup, and Kelly Services provide accounting, finance, and business systems professionals on an interim or project basis. In other words, you can rent a CFO (or three). In one case, a Robert Half client was technically insolvent. Robert Half assigned a team to analyze the situation and lay out a path to financial viability. Once the first team's work was done, a second dove in to improve business processes and information flow to speed the monthly close. This helped the client company avoid bankruptcy and set the table for recapitalization. That work allowed it to reduce its debt from $110 million to $33 million. Two years later, it was not only stable but highly profitable.[1]

Stop the Waste!

There are many midsized companies that waste boatloads of cash every month. It dribbles away on unproductive employees. It vanishes because the company is paying too much for too many things and spending money on stuff it really doesn't need. When times are good, it's easy to say that the real growth of the business comes from new products or other strategic investments. But minimizing waste is important then, too. Most businesses are valued on a multiple of EBITDA (an accounting acronym that represents the cash generated from earnings, and is defined as earnings before interest, taxes, depreciation, and amortization). Every single expense reduces EBITDA. Every company should have, as part of its culture, a disdain for wasting the company's lifeblood: its cash.

A 2011 study by CFO Research Services[2] highlights the

importance of expense management. This report followed a similar survey done in the depths of the 2009 downturn. According to the study, 86 percent of the small and midsized companies surveyed said that since 2009 they had improved their ability to manage costs. Over half said that the downturn had spurred them to develop a "less wasteful company culture."

It's wonderful how a liquidity crash can focus a business's attention on costs.

If you run, say, $200,000 per month in indirect expenses, and you reduce those costs by 20 percent (without reducing your volume of goods or services), and you did that for just twelve months, you'd save almost a half-million dollars.

Firms with solid budgeting are able to show individual leaders what they are spending. Awareness of spending is the first and most important step in reducing waste. Targets and limits can (and should) be set. Then managers (and others) can monitor their spending against those plans.

Budgets don't have to be complex or cumbersome. Often, the simpler the better, but the key is that the data collection must be valid and the actuals be compared to budget often, with adjustments made as needed.

Always Be Ready to Borrow

Once you have a budget that reflects reality, borrowing becomes a more feasible way to manage a hungry balance sheet. Of course, this requires an agreeable lender. While we can't bend the bank to our desires, at the very least we should know what its standards are and when it will likely say no. If it's going to be a no, we CEOs would always rather know quickly.

Negotiate with your bank to raise your line each year, and borrow the money long before you're in desperate need of it.

Draw up the line as business gets difficult, keeping your cash balance in a comfortable zone.

Why should you borrow before you absolutely need to? It cements your relationship with your bank. The toy importer I discussed in chapter 2 had a $15 million line of credit, and was only using half of it. When its warehouse management system implementation cratered and the company could no longer ship goods expeditiously, it was able to borrow an additional $8 million immediately, a saving grace. Its CFO, who had kept on excellent terms with the bank, then negotiated an additional $4 million unsecured "air ball" loan in early 2009—a time when getting a loan was far from easy. The fact that the business had already borrowed the money meant that when the bank called in the note in late 2010, it was stuck. The firm was worth a lot more to it alive than dead, and so the bank cooled its heels until the company recovered.

For the bank, there was no viable alternative.

Be Careful with OPM (Other People's Money)

Borrowing from a bank is one thing; borrowing from equity sources is a different kettle of fish. Owners have a duty to properly capitalize a business or step up to invest if needed. Owners may be the proprietors, a set of partners, professional investors (venture capital or private equity), or stockholders in the public markets. At any of these levels, having the wrong owners can either stir up a liquidity crash or make one more difficult to deal with. Partners squabble, individual owners and VC funds run out of money. Even public firms might have to manage flighty investors who flee at the first sign of trouble, sinking the stock price. They may have to deal with activist investors who pressure boards to change strategy or management.

The moral here is to choose your owners and investors with care. Once they're in place, they can be quite hard to change.

In many closely held businesses, owners are also the management. The separate roles have separate responsibilities, but many owners do not understand the distinction. A split mind-set on the board is bad news. Investors who want different outcomes—some going long and others planning quick exits—can prevent a company from developing a unified strategy for dealing with a liquidity crash.

Long before you find yourself in a liquidity crash, think about who should and should not be your investors. Here is a quick primer on the three most common categories of investors.

Common Types of Investors

- **Angel investors** are moderately wealthy individuals who like to invest in very young companies, often in increments of $50,000, typically up to $500,000. They often wind up on the board, or coach the CEO or founder to help him grow the business. Some angels are very business savvy. Some are not.

- **Venture capitalists** (**VCs**) are firms led by professional investors who raise money from wealthy individuals or institutional investors (acting as limited partners) and look to invest those funds in companies that are high growth, high risk. These companies might fail, or they might become hugely valuable and (ideally) go public. VCs are looking for the big score, knowing that most of the companies they invest in will fail. They often invest $500,000 to $40 million (for midsized firms) and don't like to invest in steady companies or even fast-growing companies that aren't positioned to hit it extraordinarily big. VCs are willing to wait eight to ten years for their companies to become big winners.

- **Private equity firms (PEs)** also aggregate money from wealthy individuals and institutional investors. Many like to invest in midsized firms, either in minority or controlling positions. Their game plan is to invest in strong businesses, drive quick growth, and then typically sell them in three to five years for a return of two to four times their invested capital. In other words, they don't seek the high-growth, high-risk companies that VCs like. They don't expect the companies they invest in to fail. They are happy with moderate returns, often in industries with historically steady growth.

CEOs who raise money from the wrong sources (including themselves and their partners), and who don't execute on plan, or need more capital to save the business, will face a liquidity crash when the current owners either don't want to invest more cash, or can't. Then the CEO must find new investors, and those investors will have a hard time with the fact that management failed to hit its earlier forecasts. They will either pass or ask for a low valuation, which dilutes the value of earlier investments, and perhaps management's. This problem starts early, when funds are raised and money is taken without regard to whether these investors will be willing and able to step up down the road.

Closely held midsized businesses usually take OPM only when they're desperate. That's when they look to VCs, private equity firms, angels, or friends and family. And by then, it's often too late.

What's my advice on taking other people's money? Wait.

People with money to invest are selfish. That's not a bad thing. They just want a solid (or better) return on their money.

They don't necessarily share the CEO's growth dreams. They want financial results every day. Specifically, they want the return you promised them when you sought their money, and they want the return when you told them they would get it. Even people with whom you are comfortable (they may be friends) and who believe in your vision will become difficult and unhappy if they get less than the return they expected and were promised.

So before you take their money, ask yourself these three questions:

1. *Do I need it?* Life is not easy for businesses running on OPM. The money is often doled out in small lump sums, forcing you to return for more over and over. Debt has to be repaid, and the interest on the debt hurts the bottom line. Your investors will keep a close eye on your performance, too. The grass is not necessarily greener for those using OPM.

2. *Am I prepared to ask for it?* Smart money (people who invest for a living and know what they are doing) is really good at sizing up businesses and their CEOs. You can't start a conversation with them until you have a clear vision, a solid plan, and a team capable of executing it well. Your investors are entrusting their money to the CEO as well as to the business. They need to believe that the CEO has everything under control. If you don't, they'll know, and they'll show you the door pretty quickly. (Of course, having a clear vision, a good plan, and a capable team is something that you should have even if you are not looking for outside money.) And stay away from *dumb* money (lottery winners and trust-fund kids who don't know business). They may invest more easily than the professionals, but they get nervous faster, and angry faster after that, and often cause bigger headaches.

3. *Are the goals of the money source aligned with yours?* If your money source needs to exit in five years, and your timeline for success is ten, you're bound to start getting a lot of grief at the five-year mark. VC funds often have ten-year horizons, and they want a big return. Private equity firms typically look to sell their portfolio companies in three to five years at a good multiple of what they paid for those businesses. If they don't think they're going to get that multiple, they begin throwing their weight around. Banks only want low-risk borrowers and will lend you money only if you're very healthy. (These are all broad generalizations, and there are many flavors of each type of money source.) Look to raise money from deep-pocketed investors with a long-running, proven dedication to your sector. Many liquidity crashes come when investors can't or won't deliver when the business needs more capital.

For example, one VC-backed firm had a group of new investors who wanted to grow the business dramatically and then exit via an initial public stock offering (IPO). They were willing to wait. But the business's earlier investors were tired and more risk averse. They wanted to exit more rapidly by finding a buyer for the firm without further diluting their shares. Management wanted to grow the firm aggressively, even without short-term profit, but it couldn't count on the board for more investment. So the business found itself taking triangulated fire from the new investors, the old investors, and company management.

What a mess.

Closely held businesses should *always* think twice about taking money from outsiders. The ride is quite different, and the penalty for disappointing outside investors can be severe.

But even when closely held businesses don't turn outward for money, the partners need to be aligned in their appetite for risk and their ability to put money into their business. They also must share the same vision of the business and its realities, especially in a liquidity crash.

The Saving Grace of Saving

When MBH Architects began to hurt, it was fortunate that the founders had foreseen that such a problem might arise. In 2006 and 2007, when the partners each earned big bonuses, they agreed to save most of it for a rainy day. In those years of double-digit growth, it seemed like it might never rain. But when it did, and it rained heavily, Heath and McNulty were able to loan the business $500,000 each in the last two torrential weeks of December 2008.

"Like many professional services firms, we pay out our profits through bonuses to reduce corporate taxes," says MBH controller Mellows. "When you bonus everything out to the owners (and the staff as well), it's incumbent upon the ownership to maintain a balance somewhere. If you're keeping it outside the company, you have to be able to bring it back in. And that's what [Heath and McNulty] did very responsibly. Without that money, we'd be gone."

This brings us to the best source of money in a liquidity crash: your own.

Owners of midsized businesses are well-advised to preserve financial depth outside the business so they can put it back in (if they so choose) to help a worthy business through a liquidity crash. Banks lend money at low interest when risk is low. They are not usually a solution when risk is high. Keeping cash reserves (inside or outside the business) is the ultimate safety net. Public companies keep large cash reserves for just this purpose, and will cut deeply before dipping into them. Private companies, to their peril, often play much closer to the illiquidity line.

Many private firms drain the company of cash to reduce

taxes, as was the case at MBH. Yet what Heath and McNulty did (and what so many ownership groups fail to do) was save that money. They also agreed on the purpose of those savings: to protect their business. When the capital call came, they were able to write checks because they had it and believed their business was worth it.

But many midsized businesses are run by professional managers who are not shareholders. In a liquidity crash, prospective investors and even current owners will ask themselves, "Is the business worth it? Is this new investment wise?" If the answer is no, the business will end, as perhaps it should.

But the right external investors can help a company survive a liquidity crash. For example, a financial services firm was bought by a private equity firm in early 2004. Unfortunately, that fall the firm found out that when a key customer's contract would come up for renewal in 2006, the new terms would cut EBITDA by about 35 percent. With 2005 revenue of more than $100 million, the firm placed a $6 million bet on a promising new division that (it believed) would replace much of the EBITDA that would be lost. Then it placed a second $6 million bet on a second new division. By spring 2006, one bet had failed completely and the other was at breakeven with no hope of making a difference to the firm's aggregate EBITDA. And when the key customer's new terms were finally nailed down, EBITDA fell 60 percent, almost twice as much as was expected.

There was no way the firm was going to avoid a significant hit to the bottom line. It was still going to be profitable; it was not even close to posting a net loss. However, the private equity owners had fully leveraged the firm when they purchased it, and a recent recapitalization had kept it maximally leveraged. That's a great strategy for pushing up ROI in good times, but it creates turmoil when earnings decline.

While the company's borrowing was a comfortable three

times EBITDA in 2005, with the earnings hit in 2006 it soared to an untenable ten times EBITDA. Faced with an immediate breach of loan covenants, the CEO turned to the board and the private equity group that owned the company. While they weren't happy about it, they stepped in, negotiated with the bank and ultimately guaranteed some of the bank debt to reduce the lender's risk. That bought time to pull EBITDA back up.

The lesson here is that all money sources are not alike, and seasoned CEOs know that being funded by smart money is best even if it might be a bit more difficult or more costly to obtain. Smart money understands that businesses have ups and downs, and it will stay rational in difficult times. The financial firm's money was smart.

By the end of 2007, the firm had increased EBITDA by 54 percent over 2006, a huge step forward. There would be a 35 percent increase in earnings in 2008. In 2012 the firm went public, and currently reports annual revenues of more than $200 million with a 10 percent net profit margin, and a market capitalization of more than $500 million.

If the private equity group had not stepped up to the plate, it's doubtful the story would have ended nearly as well.

Early and careful planning for current and future financing sources helps keep a variety of lenders in play, giving the CEO choices. Of course, good performance on or above plan is another prerequisite for having multiple financing options in your pocket.

Being Public Is Not a Safety Net

Many CEOs of private companies believe public firms have it easier when it comes to raising capital. That's not true when the public firm is midsized.

Just like private companies, when a public company is

in trouble it is often too late to raise money. Public companies must carry a strong enough balance sheet to carry them through any difficult periods until their prospects look brighter and their market cap has recovered.

The classic liquidity crash hits a public company that has had a choppy period, and its stock price suffers, earning bad press. The firm eats into its cash reserves and the balance sheet weakens. Hedge funds or activist shareholders smell opportunity and buy in when the valuation is low, eager for a quick recovery so they can cash in. But the company doesn't bounce back. Then it takes many quarters or years to work through the problems. Wall Street analysts become critical. Normally quiet investors start to get upset, and vocal.

More capital is required to invest in growth. Debt is risky, or is not available at the scale needed. If the company tries to issue new stock to raise additional equity, shareholders may object (activist shareholders certainly will) to the dilution of their interests. Commonly, dilution of more than 10 percent causes a lot of commotion. They'll question whether the company has pursued all other options. If you didn't turn over every rock, expect costly lawsuits.

For example, before the rough times, a firm's market capitalization might have been valued at $300 million, and it likely would have been able to raise $30 million by issuing new shares. But if the market cap has slumped to $150 million, it can only raise $15 million (using the 10 percent guide). Financing through a PIPE (private investment in a public entity) usually causes similar resistance to dilution, especially if activist shareholders are present. Furthermore, putting many new shares on the open market (when demand for the stock is low) can drive the share price into the ground and bring in very little cash.

If the company can't convince its board that diluting ownership will raise enough money for a quick recovery (raising less than enough money is usually an awful idea), then the company is stuck. Boards that make decisions that irritate active shareholders tend to be voted out. Board members have reputations, and their performance is tracked by firms that supply intelligence to institutional investors. They don't want to get thrown off boards, so the loud voices (activist shareholders) have an impact greater than the shares they own.

There is always some hope that a shareholder vote will approve a capital raise, and this is almost always required if it leads to 20 percent more shares outstanding. However, it will take months to prepare and issue proxy statements with sufficient notice, solicit votes, and hold the shareholder meeting. Do you have enough cash to hold out until then, and what if you lose the vote? This is no easy deal.

Management teams (and CEOs in particular) who pursue dilutive financing may find themselves at odds with their board, which may be more focused on short-term stock performance than on the long-term health and growth of the company. And when the board and the CEO are at odds, the CEO usually loses.

Your Survival Guide in a Liquidity Crash

If you run any business long enough, you'll hit a down cycle. Welcome to the club.

Hard times can befall a business for a host of reasons. When the headlines are grim, as they were in 2008, it's easy to start panicking and running a business too conservatively. That will cause you to miss opportunities to grow. You'll under-spend in critical areas, and although you'll reduce the risk of a big cash crash, you'll increase the risk that your business will shrink.

Your goal should be to outlast the downturn (and your competition) while positioning yourself to grow when the good times return.

Surviving the downturn sometimes requires the business leader to do unpopular things to survive. Survival is a harsh business.

To prepare for anticipated hard times, you should:

• *Reduce your debt.* Having to make debt payments is really hard in lean times. The survival rate of debt-free companies is much higher.

• *Befriend your bank.* Get on the good side of your bank and enlarge your credit line. But don't use it! For debt that you'll need for a long time, use long-term loans, not your credit line. Banks won't give you loans when you're on the ropes, so you must have them in place and set up *before* you really need them.

As the downturn approaches, you want to:

• *Beef up your mission-critical infrastructure.* While you still have the money to do it, upgrade computers nearing end of life, production equipment, and other capital-intensive business infrastructure just enough. They should be solid enough that you won't need to replace them for at least two years. But don't get carried away, because you will be draining your own bank account and decreasing your flexibility down the line. MBH Architects' new data center, new offices, and phones (deployed before the downturn) made it possible for it to defer nearly all capital expenditures—and still execute at a high level—when cash was hard to find. The upgrades also allowed the company to hit the ground running when the economy improved.

• *Halt marginal programs.* These are those great ideas that turned out to be not so great. Pulling the plug on them helps the bottom line and forces you to focus on your core business.

• *Protect the owner's personal net worth.* There is a lot you can do to shield your own assets from a business failure, but only if you do so more than a year before a bankruptcy filing. Some debt is also stickier than other debt; some debt is so sticky that you can't shake it even in a bankruptcy filing. Work to pay down that kind of debt first.

• *Prepare to mitigate the damages if you crash and burn.* While small businesses often go bust and stick everyone with the bill, more is expected from midsized businesses. You may need to close the business (or sell it) while you still have millions in the bank account, enough to pay off debt or insure that customer obligations are fulfilled by others. You as CEO, and your board of directors, have legal and moral obligations to investors, banks, creditors, employees, local governments, and often customers. These obligations become more complex if you have international subsidiaries. If serious liquidity risk exists, seek professional advice.

Once the impact of a liquidity crash becomes unavoidable, the most important thing is to conserve the cash you still have. To do so, cut hard, cut fast, and:

• *Stay profitable every month.* Continuing losses will suck your business dry. Eventually, they will kill you.

• *Communicate thoughtfully and carefully with customers and vendors.* There is a delicate balance between the positives of flying below the radar screen (good) versus the negatives of hitting customers with service or delivery failures and surprising suppliers that, unprepared, may dump you at the worst time. There is an art to managing relationships under these circumstances. Be artful.

• *Don't invest.* Don't build up inventory or any other fixed assets. Only replenish what you absolutely must to continue doing business.

- *Don't spend.* Don't let your liabilities grow, especially secured liabilities or those you can never shed. Keep your credit card under lock and key. Avoid running up your line of credit and what you owe your vendors if you can possibly avoid it.

- *Sell off inventory and equipment you don't need.* Don't think you'll need them for a rainy day. It's raining now.

- *Focus on receivables and payables.* Offer select customers incentives to pay sooner. Negotiate longer terms to pay suppliers. This generates cash that's locked up in your business. And double-check your credit policies, so you carefully manage the risk of bad debt.

- *Lay off quickly.* Fire employees you don't love; if you can, keep those you do. As the work slows down, so do people. They stretch out their work to protect themselves and they'll tell you that "everyone we have is essential." That's just not true. Keep wages in line with sales volume.

- *Don't forget your customers.* You need to keep sales volume up, and finding new customers is hard, not to mention expensive. If sales volume falls too low, you'll have trouble covering your overhead. So do everything you can to keep your current customers satisfied.

- *Take (limited) risks.* All cost cutting and no growth will kill a company as surely as running out of cash. If it's possible, try some low-investment product extensions or a new promotion to certain customer groups. If you can pick up volume this way, you'll cover your overhead more easily. But please: no big bets.

- *Remember what makes you special.* What makes you special is what you do better than anyone else. Doing that will win new orders and customers. Spend your resources on that, and ignore as much of the rest as you can. And cut anything else that won't return short-term results.

Having run a business through several downturns, I can tell you that it's not much fun. Surviving a liquidity crash requires a lot of hard work. But when the cash crunch comes, you don't really have a choice. Just how badly do you want to stay in business?

Only you can answer that.

7

Tolerating Dysfunctional Leaders

I left this growth killer for last for a reason. Look over the first six silent growth killers listed below.

- Chapter 1: Letting Time Slip-Slide Away
- Chapter 2: Strategy Tinkering at the Top
- Chapter 3: Reckless Attempts at Growth
- Chapter 4: Fumbled Strategic Acquisitions
- Chapter 5: Operational Meltdown
- Chapter 6: The Liquidity Crash

Now, imagine you had the leadership team of your dreams. Incredibly experienced men and women, all ready, willing, and capable of tackling the business's challenges. Do you think these six growth killers would be as likely to victimize your company?

Of course not. Killers search out the weak, the least able to defend themselves. They don't usually choose brawny, powerful targets to attack.

Having a stellar leadership team is what makes your company strong; it is one of the pillars of leadership infrastructure. (I'll explain what I mean by leadership infrastructure more fully in my concluding chapter.) Unfortunately, many midsized company CEOs put up with dysfunctional leaders, thereby weakening their business's ability to first avoid and then fight off the growth killers.

That's why tolerating dysfunctional leaders is the seventh, and last, silent growth killer.

Tolerating dysfunctional leaders is a particularly serious problem for midsized firms. They generally don't have the luxury of a large leadership team to support weak links in the executive chain. The average midsized firm that I work with (from $20 million to $400 million in revenue) has five to ten people in the C-suite. Compare that with the forty-one corporate-level executives at Ford (a $134 billion company) or the fifteen at Western Union (at $5 billion, a much smaller company than Ford).

Two or three weak links out of thirty? Not a big problem.

Two or three weak links out of six? Big problem.

Having participated in meetings with hundreds of CEOs of midsized businesses in the last five years, I have found their most common complaint is the underperformance of their executive team members. While they tell one another to dismiss these managers quickly, they almost always postpone the firing. However, once they do the deed, we hear how a demoralized executive team, driven to despair by poor-performing peers, is suddenly reinvigorated.

My own research and consulting experience tells me that loyalty to underperforming executives is a central leadership problem at midsized companies, and one that if allowed to continue will assuredly kill a company's growth.

Struck by Lightning

Consider this example of growth killer number seven at work. In 2001, a young food manufacturer (a $30 million business today), was growing like a weed. The CEO wanted to concentrate on the company's finances and internal operations, and thought he could accelerate the company's growth at the same time by bringing in a top sales executive.

The new executive didn't want the mundane title VP of sales; he wanted to be called...the chief lightning catcher. He said if the CEO really wanted to grow sales, the chief lightning catcher would need broader authority. He presented the CEO with a forty-page employment contract. With the help of counsel, the CEO modified and signed it.

The chief lightning catcher had previously worked for the firm as a consultant, kicked open a few doors, and created a mystique about how he did what he did. The CEO believed in him.

The lightning catcher quickly wove himself into the company's corporate fabric. He dominated the sales area, and then began pushing the CEO out of it. The lightning catcher became a black box from which sales would emerge. The sales team, he made clear, was loyal to him.

Even though the lightning catcher always talked about big opportunities that were "about to break wide open," sales flattened from 2004 to 2006. But the slump was always someone else's fault. *If only the lightning catcher had more control, he could have made great strides.*

The CEO belonged to a peer group that met monthly. They had one overriding piece of advice concerning the lightning catcher: fire him. As the CEO started to think about that, the lightning catcher found a suitor for the company that would bring it some badly needed cash. Talks and due diligence followed. This was an exciting opportunity. The lightning catcher led the project and made sure that everyone knew he was indispensable to it.

But in December 2006, the Friday before Christmas, the deal fell through. The CEO later learned that it fell through because the other side wasn't comfortable with...the chief lightning catcher.

This was a big setback for the food manufacturer, but it was also a call to action. The CEO reached out to his most trusted adviser and asked him to have three lunches to develop an opinion about the lightning catcher's future: one with the CEO, one with the CEO's partner, and one with the lightning catcher.

At the end of the week, the CEO got the adviser's verdict: fire the lightning catcher.

The CEO had legal counsel review that forty-page employment contract. He created a communications plan for the day of the firing to keep the sales team calm and to communicate with customers that might be upset or have deals in process. A week before D-day, he got his top HR person involved to help coordinate the minute-by-minute details.

On May 3, 2007, at 3 p.m., he dismissed the lightning catcher.

And the CEO discovered that most of his careful preparations were unnecessary.

No one in sales even thought of quitting. They were glad the lightning catcher was gone. They had felt micromanaged.

The CEO's phone did not ring off the hook. Indeed, it hardly rang at all. The lightning catcher, it turns out, wasn't doing much communicating with customers. In fact, several customers told the CEO they had stayed with the company *despite* the lightning catcher. They were delighted he would now be catching bolts in someone else's sky.

There was a collective sigh of relief throughout the organization. No more drama. People could focus on their work. Three months after the lightning catcher's departure, the company developed a new product that became 23 percent of total sales. In five months, with the sales team reenergized, the company signed up a giant discount retailer, which grew to represent 25 percent of total sales. Although it's hard to measure, the return to a healthy culture made a real difference in sales, profits, innovation, and the work environment.

"I think we delayed our growth by at least two years (sales remained flat through 2008) because we brought the lightning catcher on board," the CEO says now. "In hindsight, it all seems so obvious, but it was really difficult to get clarity on the situation at the time."

The firm continued to grow. In June 2013, a large food company took a majority position in the firm, buying out some founder shares along with all the shares of an earlier private equity investor, who reported an excellent return on their investment. The two founders continue to lead the firm.

The lightning catcher spent six years at the firm. The CEO had known for at least half that time (at least subconsciously) that the lightning catcher was manipulative, divisive, and ineffective.

Why did he last so long?

In this chapter, I will discuss why leaders tolerate poor performance and dysfunctional leaders, and what it takes to create a team dedicated to your company's mission—a team with the focus and ability to do what it takes to grow your business.

Excuses, Excuses

In my experience, far too many leaders of midsized companies are overly tolerant of executives such as the chief lightning catcher: leaders who are not top performers and don't behave according to the values the organization holds dear.

Why is this? CEOs are generally bright and in control. You would think tolerating underperformance would be the last thing they would do. Yet they do, time and time again.

There are always excuses for avoiding the unpleasantness of holding people accountable and firing them, even people who deserve it. Here are some I've heard from the C-suite:

- "She does some things really well, and dismissing her will cost us in those areas." (Nobody could do the job better? Come on. There are lots of fish in the sea—if you fish diligently.)

- "I hate confrontation." (Everyone hates the negative stuff, but allowing people who are not performing to continue doing a poor job inevitably creates other, larger messes. It's the leader's *job* to do this work.)
- "I'll hire others to do what he can't or won't do." (That's costly—in time and money—and it never works. A person who's not doing his job creates waves throughout a department or organization that cannot be contained.)
- "If I fire this executive, he'll sue me; the costs could be huge." (If he's the type to sue for wrongful dismissal, the risk of keeping him on is probably also huge. Consult legal counsel, minimize the risks, and do the deed as intelligently and gently as you can. Don't let yourself be held hostage.)
- "We're dependent on her. Some programs will crash and burn without her." (Ditto if she quits. Dependency is always bad. Train and restructure your way out of it.)
- "Tackling the dismissal, replacement, and training will be a big distraction from pressing business matters." (True, but if you had an all-star team they'd be handling most of those pressing business matters and you'd have time to run the company.)
- "Firing him might mess up his life." (Not usually. There are other workplaces. But if you are a good sentry of your business, you will detect problems early. Tell the person where he is going wrong. Communicate your expectations and give the person a chance to improve. Don't mince words. If the person still can't deliver, he's earned dismissal. You run a business, not a shelter.)

Be done with excuses; set a new course.
I know. You're thinking, "It sounds easy, but it's not." I agree. But the damage you'll cause by inaction is massive, even if it doesn't scream at you every day.

Your best executives will get tired of dealing with this

dysfunctional member of the team. They'll leave. (Memorize the following: "You lose the best when you protect.") Meanwhile, whatever positive juice your team may possess will be sucked dry by internal politics and general negativity. The productivity of the department your dysfunctional executive leads will decline. Finally, your stature as a leader will erode as your people wonder why you continue to tolerate people like the lightning catcher.

I won't kid you. Clearing out the deadwood to improve your company's performance isn't a walk in the park. It will involve taking a hard look at the people around you, people you may think of as your friends, people who may not remain your friends after you put their performance under the lens.

Creating a high-performance leadership team may require confrontation. It means ranking your leadership team according to strategic criteria and letting them know where they stand. It will definitely demand long-term planning, and the somewhat tedious work of writing down standardized processes for getting things done, and making sure those processes are honored.

Most difficult of all, it will force you to take a long, hard look at yourself, at the kind of leader you are, and the kind of leader you're going to need to be if you want your company to grow and evolve.

But first, we'll look at how and why you got into this fix: an overwhelmed leader with a subpar team that's not enabling growth.

How Growth Can Spawn Subpar Teams

It was new to him, this feeling of helplessness. As an entrepreneur, Uwe (pronounced "Oovay") Druckenmueller, founder and CEO of CruiserCustomizing, a $15 million motorcycle parts and accessories provider, had always been able to jump in, work like crazy, and fix problems as they arose. But not now.

His company's growth depended upon the implementation of a new ERP system. By November 2006, the several-times-postponed cutover deadline had just been postponed again. (See chapter 1, "Letting Time Slip-Slide Away.") And the holiday orders had begun pouring in. Druckenmueller had been raised on a cattle ranch in Germany where "taking the bull by the horns" was taken literally, and that was his style. But even if he worked day and night, his company still couldn't fill its orders. And the business risks were mounting.

A tipping point—from entrepreneurial to professional management—always arrives if a start-up thrives. For Cruiser-Customizing, it happened at $15 million in revenue. But no matter when it comes, there's no avoiding it. Start-ups have to be led by a person who is hands-on. Given a start-up's limited resources, it can only hire as many helpers as it needs to get going. If the team does its job well, the business will grow. At some point, however, to continue growing to midsize, a business needs a team of leaders with specialized and managerial expertise.

Every leader of a small, growing business must acknowledge this fact of life, and continually think about when, and how aggressively, to modify the management team to handle growth properly.

This changeover shouldn't happen abruptly. Some of the original start-up team may be able to grow into professional managers. Others may not need to professionalize for another few years. But one staff position must lead the march: the CEO.

Super high-growth, venture capital–funded companies frequently change CEOs at the tipping point. They start by hiring CEOs who flourish in the start-up role and excel at the early-stage heavy lifting. The VCs know that as the business gets to the next level, the first CEO will leave and a new CEO, skilled at running larger firms, will step in. But most privately held firms are owned by a CEO who wants to continue running the firm he or she started.

That was Druckenmueller. With his training in software engineering, not business, he knew he had a lot to learn. He had joined the Alliance of Chief Executives two years earlier to learn from his peers. He read business books and hired a consultant to help the company make the shift, all while managing 25 percent or more annual sales growth. In 2010, Druckenmueller decided it was time to bring in an experienced CEO and step up to the chairman's role. That would allow him to focus on his growth strategy of developing an online motorcycle community.

Druckenmueller's approach was perfect. He saw the need for change, and he led that change with his own actions. Too often, CEOs react by doing more of what they did when they started the company: they work feverishly and involve themselves in every decision. However, this is a path to stagnation and missed opportunities for their businesses.

I've seen four common reasons that leaders struggle when their companies hit the tipping point:

1. **Their problems become more complex.** At one software firm, a founding team member struggled to create a strong product marketing function. He knew software, not marketing. So he hired consultants and read voraciously. But he was relieved when his CEO finally hired a VP of product marketing with years of experience in larger firms. After that, the business took off.

2. **Their managers aren't leaders.** Many managers in small companies are happy to do what the CEO tells them to do. But at the tipping point, the CEO will no longer have the time (or energy) to solve their problems for them. These CEOs need leaders who can do it on their own.

3. **Their executives lack the right skills.** In small firms, please the CEO and everything's good. But midsized firms have leadership teams that might be three to five levels deep. If your executives don't know how to run teams, or possess the specialized knowledge and skills the business now requires, the company's growth can stall.

4. **Their team isn't thinking long term.** Executives at early-stage companies enjoy getting their hands dirty. They like to execute, and everyone pitches in. But the larger the business, the more it needs planning, anticipation, strategy, and an understanding of its market (or its future market). Some executives don't like these more sophisticated business processes, finding them tedious or bureaucratic.

What Tips a Small Business into Midsized Territory?

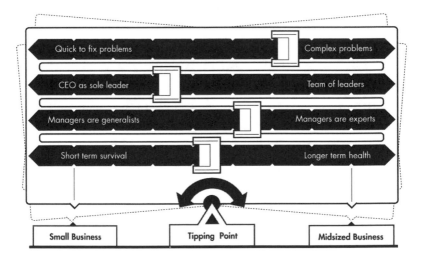

FIGURE 7-1: Not all businesses shift from small to midsized scale and behavior at the same revenue or head-count level. Move the weights on the diagram above and see if you've passed the tipping point.

Small businesses stop growing when the founder runs out of bandwidth. A few are able to leverage teams of managers to get more work done. But those businesses get stuck again at the next level, the next tipping point, when the CEO needs leaders on the top team who can lead the managers.

Changing the leadership team at the tipping point can mean cutting ties to the very people who got you there. Here's where it really gets tough.

The Loyalty Trap

Loyalty. It's a beautiful thing. In fact, it feels almost un-American to suggest that loyalty could be bad. But it can be, especially when it comes from the top of a company.

Chief executives who are loyal to their lieutenants can be enemies of growth. A company whose senior managers are coasting because once upon a time they bagged a big account or solved a big problem is a company that isn't firing on all cylinders.

Most of the leaders I know are grateful to those who helped them succeed. They develop bonds of trust and sometimes real friendships with the people they spent hundreds or thousands of hours with, working side by side. Imagine your feelings, for example, toward employee number two who endured the cold, hard years when you were all a payroll away from failure.

But past performance is no guarantee of future results.

So how do CEOs overcome the type of loyalty that leads to dysfunction? In the best-performing midsized companies, CEOs view loyalty as a checking account. Employees make deposits and withdrawals. Not doing a job well is a withdrawal. If too much time passes without new deposits, the account runs dry no matter how big it was years ago when the team member made a big deposit to open it.

Certainly, an executive who has been a solid performer over time deserves some slack for life's hiccups—a bout of illness, distraction due to a divorce, and so on. But during these times, they still are making withdrawals from their loyalty account. And while every long-term solid performer deserves coaching, guidance, and feedback so they can again achieve excellence, a medium- to long-term lack of performance almost always overdraws the loyalty account.

I've seen companies rejuvenate growth after their CEOs rethought the concept of loyalty. For example, Melanie Dulbecco has been CEO of 125-person R. Torre & Company, which makes the Torani brand syrup flavorings, for twenty years. In 2007, as growth flattened, she knew her long-standing executive team couldn't take the San Francisco–based company to the next level. In an orderly and respectful manner, she changed the team, and R. Torre has since returned to double-digit annual growth.

Was Dulbecco disloyal to those executives who had worked with her for decades? No. Dulbecco was loyal to her company's mission. Tolerating poor performers out of a sense of loyalty is ultimately disloyal to the company, and firms with active boards will hold it against the CEO. As legendary former GE CEO Jack Welch and his wife Suzy wrote in 2009: "Loyalty isn't dead, but rewarding loyalty without performance should be. It's shortsighted and wrong-headed."[1] The only loyalty that matters in business is to the success of that business.

Part of the problem with misguided loyalty is the message it sends to the whole organization: that the company or CEO is willing to compromise its values. That is a very bad message.

Healthy Loyalty Defined

Developing the right mind-set about what/ who leaders should be loyal to helps counteract the human compassion and gratefulness that many leaders feel toward past performers. Review this list carefully. Commit yourself to placing your loyalty in the right place. What/who should CEOs be loyal to?

1. High levels of performance that drive firm value.
2. Leaders who lead well and followers who follow well.
3. Strategic thinking.
4. New ideas that feed vision and innovate.
5. Risk takers.

What/who should CEOs *not* be loyal to?
1. Leaders who are not leading.
2. Past performers who are not performing now (even if they are friends or favorites).
3. Complacency and ordinary thinking.
4. Hidden agendas and actions that are toxic to the firm.
5. Low-level performers who are not destined to improve.
6. Those whose time has passed and have failed to adapt.

CEOs often wait too long to make the tough choices because they are emotionally attached to individuals in their organizations. I have been guilty of this myself, but no more.

Tolerating High-Maintenance Leaders

High-maintenance leaders can be effective in their jobs but at a high cost to the organization and their managers. My allergy to this type of leader developed as all allergies do: through repeated exposure. After twenty years of company leadership, I took the oath: no more babysitting.

High-maintenance leaders come in various flavors. There is:

Ms. Over-Her-Head. She graduated top of her class and said she wanted to be challenged so I put her in a position that would stretch her. But often she would say her job was too difficult and get upset. I spent a lot of time encouraging her and talked her out of leaving several times. Then she quit after eighteen months with no notice and no explanation. Had I accepted her resignation the first time, I would have been better off.

Mr. Angry. He was big, a martial arts black belt with good technical skills and a certain charm. He also snarled often and exploded about once a month. I became a pro at smoothing things over, and he always promised to "be better." He did improve his department's technological capabilities, but he also kept everyone on edge, which ate up quite a bit of my time and adversely affected the office's culture. The team was relieved when he moved on.

Mr. Arrogant. This CTO was convinced that he was the smartest guy in every room. He demanded weekly meetings with the CEO, insisting that all the other departments needed to change. The CEO kept talking him down, but the meetings he attended were invariably tense affairs. He got the whole management team into a twist until he left to launch his own start-up, free at last to do everything his own way. Perhaps not surprisingly, it failed.

Mr. Drama. He came in with great credentials, and had some great ideas. But cool, calm, and collected he was not. He could be counted upon to make inflammatory comments and start firestorms. Running a meeting with him present was nearly impossible. It would go off track; people would get into fights and inevitably somebody would walk out. Eventually, he blew himself out of the organization in spectacular fashion.

Ms. Hero. She made no secret that she believed the company would fall apart without her. She worked nights and weekends. She sacrificed her personal life for her work, and she made sure everyone knew it and knew how underappreciated she was. She was always in the CEO's office pleading for more responsibility, demanding that her slacker peers change their ways. Yes, she worked hard, but the price everyone had to pay was too high.

I could keep going, but I won't. All these individuals had their merits, but all required babysitting. The leader should be a lot of things, but never a babysitter. Babysitting devours time that should be devoted to building the organization.

High-maintenance members of the leadership team who don't contribute much are typically fired fairly quickly. It's the executives who are contributors (or trying to be) who stick around long enough to become problems.

We convince ourselves they're worth the trouble. We try to fix them (as we should). But when fixing them fails, we try to work around their flaws by insulating them, or isolating them, or acting as a buffer between them and others. That, we shouldn't do.

The truth is that when fixing them fails (after a well-defined, relatively short period of time), we need to cut our losses and fire them. Take the time and energy that went into babysitting them and devote it to hiring a high-output, low-maintenance replacement. They're out there. In fact, I can't recall a single instance when I didn't find a better replacement after firing a high-maintenance employee, and I've never had a client who fired a high-maintenance employee and regretted doing so.

The executive's duty is to lead the team to success. If success is important to you, be sure to select and retain great team members.

Of course, first you have to know what you have to work with.

Evaluating Your Leadership Team

As a veteran CEO, I have found that if you don't shed your high-maintenance leaders and your poor performers in favor of encouraging and developing low-maintenance high performers, you'll lose your best and most creative people.

I often see employees (including management) who aren't evaluated with sufficient rigor. These "problem children" and poor performers degrade the work environment by encouraging average performers to slack off. Then high performers either leave (they prefer working with other high performers) or become demotivated and hard to manage.

One key to improving performance is to reduce the range between the lowest and highest performers. Much research has been done in this area by Elkiem, a firm that's been investigating and analyzing high-performance environments for more than twenty years.

In high-performance environments, poor performers feel uncomfortable. They get counseling, encouragement, and tough evaluations. This either nudges them to perform at higher levels or encourages them to leave. The company is left with higher average performers and a tighter performance range.

With the lowest performers gone or improved, new people—who used to be average—are now on the low end of the scale, and feel pressured to perform at higher levels.

A few caveats come with this process. A company that applies too much pressure will lose good people. Further, if the metrics for performance aren't understood and accepted by all, the environment becomes confusing and harsh, and great people will leave. People must know what is required of them to be successful. Without that clarity, the path to winning becomes political—making friends with the right people—and performance is bound to suffer.

In my consulting work, I have some CEO clients who are fond of everyone in their leadership team and rarely reprimand or fire poor-performing leaders. In these cases, I sometimes will urge the CEO to rank his leadership team. In my own company (I was CEO for twenty-three years), executives at times would want to give equal raises to their whole team. I would require them to rank their team and, based on that, justify the pay level of each person. This encouraged them to take a harder look at their team, and it drove better decision making.

Leaders of midsized companies must evaluate people based on clear criteria. They then must reward the high performers and get the poor performers to improve or leave.

But what are the criteria on which to rate your leaders? I suggest you ask yourself these six questions annually about each of your leaders, or jump online at www.ceotoceo.biz/ mightytools.html to see how your leadership team stacks up.

1. Is this person an ideal person who will significantly help pull the company to the next level?
2. Would you hire this person now, if he wasn't already on board?
3. Draw the organizational chart of the future (boxes with no names). Are you eager to place this person in that org chart—given the size the firm will be in a few years?
4. Assess this person's strengths not as an individual contributor, but as a team player and as a leader of her team.
5. Has he traveled the road ahead at a prior job? If not, is he a voracious learner?
6. How has she been rated by her peers, on her 360 ratings?

Listen to how you answer these questions, then take action. Repair your worst performers or replace them.

The Leader Without Portfolio

I asked him for his secret for staying at the top of the rocket that is his company. He said, "I'm not that introspective." Nonsense.

Dan Warmenhoven, former chairman and CEO of NetApp, grew a $15 million firm to $6 billion in nineteen years and is quite introspective, as a leader must be. He thinks about who he is, what he stands for, and why he does what he does all the time.

Of course, right after he said he's not introspective, he gave us all some clues to his internal processes at a meeting of the Alliance of Chief Executives.

NetApp makes giant data storage units—cabinets full of disk drives—for big organizations. Warmenhoven joined the firm as CEO in 1994. It grew at 45 percent year over year on average for every year of its existence. It self-funded the growth by getting vendors to finance their inventory. The company focused on one area and dominated it with a leading product. But what interested me most were the leadership and business lessons Warmenhoven provided.

Yes, that's what he said. He tries never to own any task. If something needs to be done, it is assigned to someone on the management team. Warmenhoven keeps himself task-free to follow his instincts and dive into any area where he feels he can add value. Sometimes, he digs into new opportunities. He spends much of his time in the field. By keeping out of the day to day, he is able to stay ahead of the company's incredible growth.

I can see doing that when I run a $2 billion company, even a $500 million company. But what about a $3 million to $50 million midsized firm? Can such an organization build a top team so fully capable of handling the day to day that the CEO can be jobless?

Every CEO I know (including me) would be delighted to have a top team so competent, so seamless in their interaction that he didn't have to worry about the day-to-day operation of the business. But almost none of the CEOs I know have such a team.

At NetApp, Warmenhoven says that every person (manager and nonmanager) is interviewed ten times before the hiring decision is made. The three must-haves they look for are 1) a desire to collaborate—especially when faced with ambiguous situations, 2) an eagerness to assume responsibility, and 3) evidence that they have done excellent work in the past.

If you hire carefully so you only get great people and send your mistakes packing quickly, you will end up with a team that is eager to do your job for you, and will do it well, leaving you jobless like Warmenhoven.

Warmenhoven calls his top team "a herd" (and means it as a compliment) because they all have similar values and ethics and they've worked together for a very long time. Consequently, they don't need endless meetings to communicate; they don't waste time jockeying for position and they always pull in the same direction. They finish each other's sentences.

Not surprisingly, Warmenhoven says his biggest concern is maintaining the quality of the people leading NetApp. I'm pretty sure he's referring to thousands of employees, because when you grow that fast everyone has to lead. At the top, Warmenhoven says, "We set the goals, we set the budgets, and we let the teams figure out how to get there."

Maybe Warmenhoven was just introspective enough to figure out the importance of building a high-performance team that would free him to deploy his talents where they added the most value. Or maybe he was just lucky for eleven years, lucky enough to pilot an IT firm through the bursting of the Internet bubble and subsequent IT industry collapse in 2001. (NetApp lost 70 percent of its customer base in one year.)

Lucky? I doubt it.

Instead of hoping to get lucky, get introspective. For the next ten minutes, do nothing but think about yourself and your top team. Is everyone, including you, doing the things that will support your company's growth? Figure out what you need to do to make the answer yes. Then get cracking.

Repair or Replace

I write this section with some hesitation. Too many leaders try, try, and try again to repair problem leaders, only to end up firing them after expending a great deal of time and emotional energy while putting their organizations through the wringer. My message is to move quickly to change out bad leaders. Only try to repair them if these three factors apply:

1. They're hungry for it. Don't even bother to start a repair effort unless the subject has acknowledged the problem (fully) and is eager to improve. In many cases, problem leaders think they're fine just the way they are and agree to work on things to "fit in." If you sense this attitude, fire right away. Real change takes work. It will be uncomfortable. Only try to repair underperforming leaders if you feel they genuinely want to change.

2. They're capable. Even with the desire and readiness to do the hard work change requires, some leaders just don't have what it takes. This is a painful conclusion to come to, and it's especially hard to communicate your assessment to the individual. Making a decision on this critical point is important for both the company and the individual.

For the company, if the leader doesn't have it, you'll waste valuable resources on a futile effort, and when you ultimately pull the plug it, may be viewed as cruel by others in the organization since the leader "was trying so hard."

As for individual leaders, you will have raised their hopes only to dash them, making them feel like a failure. If their attitude is great but the ability is lacking, I'm a big fan of pointing the person toward other challenges in the company to which he may be more suited and where he can succeed. If that isn't possible, dismiss in as kind a manner as possible and move on.

3. They just need mentoring. I'm privileged to have extremely smart and talented leaders as clients. Yet they hire me to mentor them because they know they don't know everything they need to know to succeed. So too, with your own leaders.

If you've decided to repair a leader, you must make the commitment to coaching and mentoring, and the leader's number one mentor must be you. You must model the desired behaviors. You must provide feedback on every behavior you seek in a member of the team. Too often, I see projects tossed over the fence to subordinates with no time allotted for supervision or feedback. Then, when subpar work is done, the top leader is indignant at the subordinate. Wrong!

For example, one director-level leader was very upset when a manager reporting to him kept stalling on hiring a supervisor. I asked the director if the manager had ever hired anyone before. He hadn't. I suggested that this first hire could be done in tandem with the director so the manager could see how it's done. The project and all subsequent hires moved forward quickly after that.

Don't Confuse Titles with Competencies

CEOs often get frustrated when they ask a person with director-level abilities to assume executive-level responsibilities.

Small firms usually start with one executive: the CEO, surrounded by helpers. Often, supervisor- or manager-level staffers that do what they are told, with some level of autonomy. Yet as a firm enters midsize, the CEO needs several director-level leaders who can manage bigger chunks of work with less direction, thereby freeing up the CEO. As most firms cross $10 million in revenues, they need at least one executive-level leader (in addition to the CEO) who can understand the company's needs broadly, and can tackle them with very little guidance. Yet promoting someone and bestowing a new title doesn't make her capable.

Here are some descriptions of common managerial positions and duties:

• Supervisor—Deals with individuals and tasks. People are directly and solely responsible to the supervisor. The supervisor may or may not have hire/fire/salary authority, but certainly should be involved in those decisions. And the supervisor gets to say what someone *must* do, as opposed to a coordinator, who tells people what they *should* do.

• Manager—Deals with groups and priorities. A manager allocates resources to the most important projects and initiatives. Managers take a tactical perspective with initiatives defined by directors and VPs and make them happen. A key skill managers must possess is the ability to get things done. Therefore, they should be measured by results. They make timely and effective hire/fire decisions.

• Director—Bestowing this title should be a really big deal (as should the VP title). This is a person who thinks about where the company is going, and the strategies for getting his function to support the company's objectives. Directors should have a sense of mission, some vision, and be able to add energy to the system. Directors help set operational KPIs (key performance indicators) and targets, either themselves, or collaboratively with the managers.

• Executive—In midsized firms, I'd call Jim Collins' Level Four leader[2] an executive. An executive has initiative, sees the big picture, and thinks with the entire company in mind (not just her department). She spends most of her time leading leaders, developing company-level strategy, and making high-stakes judgment calls.

The point is to match your expectations to the leader's capabilities. Most frustrated, overworked CEOs I know suffer because they don't have as many real executives around them as they need. They are trying to do the work of three executives. If you starve the leaders below you of time and attention, they stop developing and become ineffective.

It is fun watching a leader develop and grow. And I believe businesses have an obligation to help their people learn; our society needs this. But if your company is under pressure to change, the odds are low that any given leader you employ can grow at a pace that matches your company's needs. If his position is mission critical, and he is a significant distance from being ideal, repair may not be advisable.

Then it's time to replace him. And that means doing the best possible job of recruiting and hiring.

Recruit the Right People in the First Place

As the U.S. economy thaws, some of your executives—often the best ones—will jump ship, tempted by greener pastures. And as your business grows, you'll need to upgrade your leadership team and maybe add to it. There are few tasks as important as recruiting the best executives for your top team. From formulating your strategy until the last day of onboarding, you, as the CEO, must invest the time and money it takes to do it right. If you don't, I can guarantee future sleepless nights as you wrestle with all the problems that the wrong executives will cause.

Here are the top ten elements of an effective hiring strategy:

1. **A future focus.** Your recruiting process begins before you start the actual search. You need to ask yourself what you want your organization to look like next year and the year after that. What kind of executives will you need when you are a much larger company? Those are the executives you'll want to find and hire now. Executives drive growth. Write a forward-looking position specification.

2. **A large pool.** CEOs and top teams should always be on the lookout for potential executives. Right now, they may be working for the competition, for a supplier or a customer, or they might have been on your last company's top team. Continually building and maintaining a network of potential team members is one of the fastest, most reliable, and lowest-cost methods of creating a great team.

3. **A swift process.** Slow searches are a big problem. It's hard to maintain focus on hiring the right executive over a long period of time. Meanwhile, the work the new hire should be doing languishes. Worse, you may end up with only one average candidate and no other options. Diving into the process wholeheartedly gives you the best chance of filling the position quickly and having excellent choices from which to select.

4. **An appropriate salary.** The salary and bonus of a top executive will always be smaller than the cost of a poor executive's mistakes or the loss of potential profits due to subpar performance. So why wouldn't you pay that extra 10 percent or 20 percent if it means attracting superior talent? You get what you pay for, and you should *expect* to get what you pay

for. If the person you hire turns out to be ho-hum, send him packing quickly.

5. **A good career fit.** Take the time to make sure that the candidate's career path is aligned with your company's future. For example, if your new CFO needs to lead the effort to take a company public as a career move (having supported such an effort in the past), and your company is IPO-bound, that's a great fit. Without excellent alignment, your relationship with your new executive hire often will be short-lived.

6. **A good person.** A supercharger for a CEO is having interesting, stimulating, fun executives. A good hire is like candy, not medicine, for the CEO. If someone gives you an icky feeling, don't hire him, even if the resume says he's great.

7. **A consensus.** Management is a team sport, and the team has to accept the newcomer. Therefore, the team should be deeply involved in the process. Before you tie the knot with a new executive, your top team should feel comfortable with your choice. One CEO I spoke with spent three days at the company he had been asked to lead before agreeing to come aboard, conducting three- and four-hour meetings with board members and key executives to make sure they were comfortable with him.

8. **A nightmare list.** One way to get to yes is to flush out all the worries, objections, and concerns that might make both parties hesitate. I call it the nightmare list. In some cases, discussing what each person fears could go wrong will make it obvious that everyone should walk away—and that's a successful outcome. In other cases, a new level of understanding and trust may be established, and the hire can go forward.

9. **A high standard.** Too many times CEOs hire the best person they've found, not the ideal person. That's a shame. Some ways to avoid settling include having multiple candidates at the decision point from which to choose. That means hiring before you are desperate to fill the position, and doing the search in a hard and fast manner so you have the time and energy to re-start and do it over again.

10. **A robust onboarding process.** Is there a bigger crime than hiring great executives and then ignoring or undermanaging them during the critical onboarding phase? In those first ninety days, if your new executive is left to struggle needlessly, enough toxins can be created to poison even the perfect hire.

Every CEO wants an all-star team. *Employing these ten processes and techniques will help you get one.*

It's All Hard, But It's All Worth It

You go to work every day. Isn't it awful to dread what that day may bring? Wouldn't it be wonderful to wake up every morning looking forward to the day's possibilities for growth—personal, professional, and corporate?

Of course it would. Unfortunately, far too many top executives spend their days and nights in dread, white-knuckling the job. Why? Because they're supported (or, rather, not supported) by a dysfunctional team that is unable to help them take their business or function to the next level. Because they shrink from doing the hard, often unpleasant work of making sure that the people they work with, the people upon whom their own and their company's success depends, share their values and their work ethic.

And it *is* hard work. As we've seen in this chapter, creating a team willing to do whatever it takes to grow sometimes requires taking a hard, unsentimental look at people with whom you may have had close, long-term personal relationships. They may be your friends. You may lose some of them.

Creating a high-performance leadership team requires intense analysis of other people's performance. It may lead to equally intense confrontations as you try to get them to raise their game. It usually demands long-term strategic planning, and creating written, standardized processes for getting things done, as well as relentless evaluation of their performance going forward.

Hardest of all, it usually demands that you decide who *you*

Are You Pulling Your Leadership Team into the Future, or Are They Pulling Your Business for You?

FIGURE 7-2: Are you the leader toiling day after day but still losing the race, resentful of your subpar team? Or are you excited by the progress your amazing team delivers with you at their side? The choice is yours.

are, and where *your* true loyalties lie. Change is always tough. Changing yourself is double-tough.

But if you're tough enough, if you can build that team and reinvent yourself, you can be freed to follow your instincts as your company thrives precisely because you have that freedom.

Wouldn't that be nice?

You can do it. Be mighty.

Conclusion
Becoming a Mighty Midsized Company

Life would be a lot easier if each of the seven growth killers we've discussed in this book acted independently. Then we'd only have to defend ourselves against them one at a time. But the truth is that they're highly related. One can trigger another in a catastrophic cascade. But there's a silver lining. Because the growth killers all feed off one another, taking just a few preventive steps can reduce a midsized company's vulnerability to all of them.

But first, let's look at a midsized toy importer (mentioned in chapters 3 and 4) that managed to survive all seven: "Letting Time Slip-Slide Away," "Strategic Tinkering at the Top," "Reckless Attempts at Growth," "Fumbled Strategic Acquisitions," "Operational Meltdown," "Liquidity Crash," and "Tolerating Dysfunctional Leaders."

Toy Story: No Laughing Matter

This healthy toy importer boasted $70 million in revenue in 2008. It had almost no debt and its pretax profits were a fairly consistent 10 percent. The business was born in 1976, and the original founder still owned and ran the business, selling to relatively small chains and independent toy stores. Its growth was slow but steady, ranging from 1 percent to 3 percent per year.

This was a cash machine. But was this firm mighty?

Then, early in 2008, the company's CEO got some bad news. One of his customers, a small chain, had started importing its own toys. Worse, it wasn't importing them just for its own stores; it intended to supply other retailers. It intended to become a competitor.

When the upstart chain began importing its own toys, the toy importer's revenue instantly dropped $1.5 million, and that meant its growth would be negative in 2008. Naturally, the CEO wasn't happy about that, but he was more worried about the firm's future. If one chain could import its own toys, perhaps others could, too. And what if the chain started stealing his customers? The company's market share had suddenly become smaller, and it could become smaller still.

A few weeks later, the CEO made two momentous decisions. The company would begin acquiring small toy retailers to guarantee itself a customer base, and it would start selling to mass merchants to grow the top line. The CEO began shopping for a retailer to acquire. And to prepare to start selling to bigger stores, he kicked off a project to fully automate his distribution center by installing a state-of-the-art warehouse management system (WMS).

In other words, he had began tinkering with his company's long-standing and successful strategy (not usually a good idea, as we saw in chapter 2) in what would prove to be a reckless attempt at growth (chapter 3).

With the help of his longtime VP of IT, the company selected a WMS, and the CEO decided to lead the implementation, with his internal IT team building the interfaces and implementing the software. They set the cutover date for September 2008. That would be just about when their small and midsized retail customers would begin gearing up for the holiday season.

Now, implementing a WMS is nearly as difficult as

implementing an ERP system, and the impact of a WMS failure may be even more damaging. If your ERP doesn't work, you can go back to spreadsheets in accounting or figure out workarounds in the other functions the ERP touches. If your WMS doesn't work, product simply cannot go in or out the door. The IT VP had never implemented a system on the scale of a WMS, but the CEO knew him, liked him, and had faith that he could pull it off. And the CEO would oversee the project.

How hard could it be? After all, they had months to get it done. It's easy to see that, as the CEO assessed the project's requirements, he was sowing the seeds that would flower into the growth killer discussed in chapter 1, letting time slip-slide away.

Once the WMS decision was finalized, the CEO increased the pace of his search for a toy retailer to acquire. In summer 2008, he found someone looking to sell his $6 million chain. The two men bonded. The CEO began to think that if word got out about his move into retail, his customers might have second thoughts about buying from a distributor that would soon become a competitor. So, wanting to keep the deal on the down-low, and fearing leaks, the CEO decided not to engage anyone to do external due diligence on the retailer. He also pooh-poohed his CFO's advice to conduct an audit. That would take too long, the CEO said. He wanted to move quickly. It might also breach the trust he'd developed with the retailer. (Did I mention that this was the CEO's first acquisition? It was.)

He bought the ten-store chain for $4 million in August 2008. A $6 million chain for $4 million? The CEO thought he had gotten a deal.

But as soon as the papers were signed and the CFO got his first look at the chain's books, it became horrifyingly clear that it was losing money every month. And because the company's accounting was a mess, it was impossible to tell where the losses were coming from. Naturally, the retailer didn't have a decent controller, so there was no help coming from that quarter.

This is what can happen (as we discussed in chapter 4) when you fumble a strategic acquisition.

But the retailer's losses, disturbing though they might be, were not as large or immediate a problem as the WMS implementation. That was a mess, troubled and behind schedule. But Christmas was coming and the CEO figured the holiday sales spike would help his new retail arm offset its losses. Discovering their root cause could wait. Pretty much everything except the WMS could wait.

In mid-August, the CFO sounded the warning on the WMS. With a month to go before the designated cutover, more than 50 percent of the integration work (between the WMS and the company's other IT and physical systems) had been neither completed nor tested. The CFO begged the CEO not to attempt the cutover until after the holiday season. But the CEO wanted to begin selling to the giant retailers by the start of the new year. To do that, he needed the WMS and he needed it in September. And he believed in his VP of IT. He'd known him for years. He'd make it all work.

But he couldn't. Come the September cutover, the warehouse couldn't accept shipments because the bar code interface wasn't operational. In fact, there was a long list of essential system functions that wouldn't work. The toys sat in their shipping containers, filling up the company parking lot. Customer orders couldn't ship because the WMS couldn't interface with inventory. Not that that mattered so much; even if it could, the order pullers wouldn't be able to find anything, as the inventory system location module had not been installed.

The toy importer's customers were more than angry; they were frantic. Their high season, the few months upon which their whole year's profits were based, was right around the corner and their toys were sitting in a parking lot.

Actually, the parking lot was full. The company had to throw up a new warehouse to contain the overflow.

Meanwhile, the IT VP was coding as fast as he could but he really didn't know how to get the WMS up and running. The VP of distribution was also stuck. Staring at those unpacked containers, with no visibility into inventory, he threw up his hands. What could he do?

Now the CEO was beginning to feel the effects of our seventh growth killer as he experienced what happens when one plunges into a major project with a dysfunctional team such as the executives we described in chapter 7.

With the company's leadership at a total loss, inventory piling up, hundreds of enraged customers calling, and billings hitting record lows, the CEO authorized fully manual shipments. The company hired temporary workers and signed off on unlimited overtime. The temps went from container to container, digging out toys and shipping them, even if that meant only partially fulfilling the orders. Of course, people (especially temps) make mistakes, and the wrong goods were often shipped to the wrong retailers. Panicked, customers started ordering from other importers, the company's competitors, in an attempt to save their season. Others cancelled their orders.

It was chaos, and now our company was in the middle of a full-blown operational meltdown (chapter 5).

With all these growth killers battering the business, it was no time to be cheap. The company began spending money to stop the bleeding. The cost of overtime and the temporary workers came to $1.8 million over three months. To keep its customers, the company refunded shipping charges to the tune of $1.7 million.

But that was just money it spent on top of what it had already lost. The acquired chain, which cost $4 million, had itself lost $180,000 in the three months the toy company owned it. The WMS cost $500,000, and the new warehouse the company had to build after the parking lot filled up cost $800,000.

Meanwhile, accounts receivables skyrocketed, reaching $11 million above normal. Angry customers weren't inclined to pay for toys they had received too late to sell. And inventory that couldn't be shipped was $4 million above its average before the operational meltdown.

With revenue vanishing, the company turned to its line of credit, which for decades had only been lightly used. It quickly maxed out at $15 million. The CFO managed to persuade the bank to grant an additional $4 million unsecured line to keep the company afloat. He did a good job considering that providing the bank with the balance sheet was tricky, as inventory wasn't being recorded by the system because it was now largely manual, and the company's invoicing was late and inaccurate.

All the growth killers had now merged to form chapter 6's liquidity crash.

And the anticipated growth all this was about? By the beginning of 2009, that was a distant memory.

The CFO battled the liquidity crisis throughout 2009. He also found a WMS consultant to tame the operational meltdown. The WMS was up and the warehouse functioning in October 2009, a little over a year past the deadline.

Only then could the CFO turn his attention to the toy chain his CEO had bought more than a year before. He hired a second (and competent) controller for the chain in August 2010 to figure out why it was losing money. Before he could, the toy company's bank called in its loan, in October 2010. But as no other bank was interested in loaning the company any money, and as it was making its interest payments, its bank was on the hook and had little choice but to come along for the ride.

After studying the problem for a year, in November 2011 the new retail controller started closing bad stores in bad locations. The bleeding began to slow and finally stopped. In the three years since the acquisition, the retailer's losses came to $2 million. Added to the $4 million acquisition price, the total effective investment (and cash drain) was $6 million.

In 2012, the toy company's revenues were $52 million, $18 million less than they had been in 2008 when it changed its core strategy to pursue growth. Its acquired retail arm accounted for $3.5 million of that revenue, or $2.5 million less than what the chain had been generating before it was acquired. By fall 2013, the firm finally paid back all its short-term bank debt, with only a mortgage remaining.

A sad tale, indeed. Instead of reaping what it had been earning before the acquisition and WMS—$7 million in pre-tax cash flow every year for six years (from 2008 through 2013), or $42 million in total—by acquiring the wrong retailer and bungling the automation of its warehouse, all the toy importer achieved was a reduction in its top line of 26 percent without generating any free cash flow at all.

That's an impressive amount of growth killing. It's a wonder the company survived.

Leadership Infrastructure: A Prerequisite to Mightiness

It didn't have to go that way for our toy company. Experienced leaders would have seen the acquisition growth killer coming. They wouldn't have made an acquisition without performing due diligence. Empowered CFOs would have looked at the books. IT executives who have implemented complex systems like the WMS would have foreseen the difficulties and delays.

But our toy importer didn't have a CEO who knew about acquisitions, a powerful CFO, or an experienced IT leader.

Hence, the seven growth killers could creep up silently and do their dirty work unimpeded.

Knowing about the seven growth killers certainly is a good start to defending against them. When each rears its ugly head, you can spot it sooner and whack it into submission. The toy company, for all its difficulties, whacked all seven and, against all odds, survived. It's a whack-a-mole champion, for sure.

But playing whack-a-mole every day is both exhausting and unrewarding. *And while you're whacking, you're not growing.*

The bigger the firm, and the faster it grows, the more severe the challenge each growth killer presents. Think of Newton's second law of motion: Force = Mass × Acceleration. A tiny, fast-growing company has less mass, so the force of the growth killers is minimized. Its capital requirements, for example, are small, so a liquidity crash (if it doesn't kill it quickly) will be short-lived. A small company doesn't do a lot of things, so an operational meltdown is containable. Its processes are light, flexible, changing as needed, so strategy tinkering is more the norm and therefore less disruptive.

Similarly, a slow-growing $70 million–revenue firm (like our toy company) can get slammed hard and still survive because that slow growth allows it the time to adjust, albeit while suffering heavy losses. The toy company could borrow money to see it through its liquidity crisis. It had a large enough customer base. And although its revenue declined, it didn't flat-line. But a $300 million–revenue firm growing at 60 percent per year—look out! That's a lot of mass, a lot of acceleration, and therefore a lot of force when the growth killers hit.

The seven growth killers tend to prey on unprepared companies of a size and growth rate that makes them vulnerable. And that's the typical midsized company that has grown from a smaller organization that didn't have (or need) what I call leadership infrastructure. That's the corporate equivalent of the physical infrastructure that keeps society going.

Midsized Businesses Grow and Get Unruly

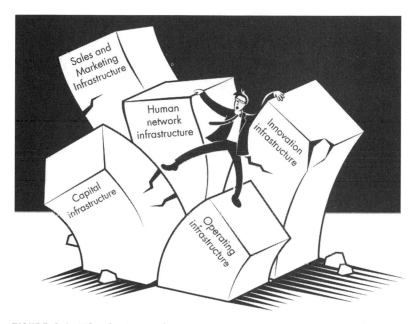

FIGURE C-1: The business has grown, and no matter how fast or strong, the founder cannot keep it all together. Help is needed.

As a society, our physical infrastructure consists of the structures that support us: roads, bridges, water pipes and pumps, sewers and generators, cellular towers, and the acres of servers and miles of wires that give us the Internet. These structures sustain us, delivering what we need to survive and thrive. They are interconnected. They are necessary. Without them, we're back in the seventeenth century. We're craftspeople and farmers.

In business, leadership infrastructure is the sum total of all the management systems, processes, leadership teams, skill sets, and disciplines that enable companies to grow from small operations into midsized or large firms. Leadership infrastructure is every bit as real as roads and bridges, electrical grids, and the Internet. Without them, we're Mom and Pop, and that's all we ever will be, no matter how much cash flow we generate.

Without leadership infrastructure, growing companies can be victimized by their own success. When they get the growth they so desperately seek, they just as quickly outgrow their leadership infrastructure. That will make the business chaotic and inefficient. Unfortunately, business schools don't teach classes in building leadership infrastructure, and it is not a natural skill for most executives. Many midsized company leaders equate it with big-company bureaucracy. That's wrong. To grow from small to big, you *must* build a leadership infrastructure.

How do you do that? Leadership infrastructure includes these four elements:

1. Quality leadership with deep experience. It includes the board of directors, the management team, subject matter experts, and consultants.

2. Planning and governance processes that ensure leaders of the company stay on track, executing a thoughtful strategy. This includes forecasting, budgeting, and performance management systems.

3. Information gathering and analytics acumen that looks externally at markets, competition, and the company's reputation, and internally at the organization's culture, teams, and performance levels.

4. An effective communications rhythm among leaders, between management and employees, and out to customers and partners.

Midsized firms may possess some or all of these elements of a leadership infrastructure, but it doesn't mean that they are as effective as they must be.

For example, between 2004 and 2007, after a first private equity–fueled acquisition of an $8 million platform company, Weymouth, Massachusetts–based air charter company JetDirect (mentioned on page 116) purchased a dozen more smaller charter operations, rolling them up to create a $200 million business, then bought $300 million TAG aviation to become a half billion–dollar firm. But the company failed to build either the systems or the management team—the leadership infrastructure—capable of integrating the acquisitions and effectively running a firm that big. Consequently, customers used to concierge-level attention grew unhappy with Jet-Direct's relatively sloppy service. Incorrect invoices were sent out; customers refused to pay them. The company hit a liquidity crash. In 2009, JetDirect's bank seized control, and two months later filed for liquidation.

What made JetDirect different from the toy company? Why did it perish while the other survived?

Partly, the toy company was lucky. And partly, it was not looking to accelerate growth to the phenomenal extent Jet-Direct was. Without stronger leadership infrastructure, there was no way that JetDirect could have walked away alive from its liquidity crash.

I'm not suggesting that every company should invest in building out its leadership infrastructure. Our toy company had sufficient leadership infrastructure to grow at 1 percent to 3 percent per year while sticking to its core business. It was only when it decided to gun for rapid growth and develop a new business model that its leadership infrastructure was revealed to be inadequate to the task. Small companies that stay small never need much leadership infrastructure.

Midsized companies that are not trying to grow quickly (and that are running profitably) probably have the leadership infrastructure they require.

But midsized companies with high growth rates, or high growth aspirations, will be pummeled by the seven growth killers if they don't strengthen their leadership infrastructure as their business grows.

How do you know your leadership infrastructure is lacking? Listen. When I hear complaints like these, I know:

- "We held a strategic off-site for the first time, but no one seems accountable for delivering on the big ideas we came up with."
- "We made what looked like a great acquisition, but it has been a headache ever since, sucking up money and all our bandwidth."
- "Our CEO is coming up with new ideas all the time, pulling people off their jobs to work on his projects, making us miss deadlines."
- "We have two executives who saved our bacon a few years back, but now that we're larger, they seem lost."
- "Two million dollars in cash used to be plenty, but not anymore; we run too low too often."
- "With so many people involved in each decision, we waste a lot of time in meetings and miss our deadlines."
- "The CEO sticks his nose into everything. Even some of our best execs have given up and just ask the CEO to tell them what he wants them to do."
- "Our CEO wants us to lead our function at a high level, but he also wants us to manage every little detail like he used to do. We don't have the time to do both well."

If you listen hard, all our seven silent growth killers lurk inside those complaints, and they all speak to a lack of leadership infrastructure. If you've heard them, your company's leadership infrastructure is inadequate. And you probably already know it. But why is building it so hard for leaders of midsized firms?

The Midsized Quandary

One reason building a leadership infrastructure is difficult for the leaders of midsized companies is because it's probably the first time they've needed it. At start-ups and small firms, leaders handle most of the detail work personally; they don't have big teams. Even the CEO is at ground level, kicking the copier when it gets stuck, making sales calls. Eventually, if things go well, the CEO will acquire a merry band of (generally) young and (usually) cheap helpers. But he will still have to tell them what to do and how to do it. Survival is the prime directive for a start-up; there's no budget for overhead or time to think of the long term. At the beginning, the business has to stay lean, with little leadership infrastructure.

Big firms already have combined a strategic, visionary C-suite with a cadre of solid, experienced middle managers who make sure the work gets done. They already possess trained workers who follow defined processes with clear instructions. Big firms are rich in leadership infrastructure. The myriad business books aimed at big companies assume that a significant leadership infrastructure is already in place. Their focus is on managing, leveraging, and improving it. But those books won't help midsized firms build their leadership infrastructure from scratch, with very little time and few resources.

Thus, midsized firms must design and build their own leadership infrastructure. But that's not easy. There's no one-size-fits-all infrastructure out there, no template. The requirements of a $10 million business are quite different from those of a $75 million or $250 million business. Even leaders who come from big companies are not always successful building a leadership infrastructure in midsized companies. They tend to overinvest, making it overly bureaucratic. Then it hinders growth instead of supporting it.

Many CEOs try piecemeal approaches based on books they read, or bits of advice they collect from peers or other advisers. But their organizations are used to doing things the old way. Getting an organization to make fundamental changes in the way it operates is one of the most difficult tasks a leader can undertake.

That's when the temptation to call in the big consulting firms to build it for you becomes especially strong. But the majority of consulting firms have big companies in mind. These consultancies are accustomed to large, rigid systems that are cumbersome to implement and even harder to maintain and govern. It isn't easy to shrink down their advice (or fees) for a midsized firm. One $20 million firm, for example, tried to follow its consulting firm's plan by creating a more rigorous business planning process. It started well, but after three planning cycles the detailed and far-reaching process was so time-consuming that it left too little time to run the business. The pendulum swung the other way with a vengeance. The company eventually went eighteen months without any plan at all.

Some midsized firms try to act big and small at the same time. Their CEOs still obsess over every detail, constantly changing direction while proclaiming big strategic imperatives, but never focusing on them. Still other times, they abandon their small-company agility and set long-term objectives without the resources they need to achieve them. Worse, they demand big-company project management skills from a loyal team that simply doesn't have them.

Midsized company leaders should look at their company's needs for leadership infrastructure holistically to try to picture what the company will need in one or two years. They should assess past performance to guide them, and tackle the work in phases.

In fact, let's imagine rewinding time to 2007 for our toy importer and see how active management of the leadership infrastructure might have produced better results. We'll need to start a year before early 2008 when the CEO made his two momentous decisions. He knew his industry was changing, since retailers importing directly from China had been a trend since the late 1990s, and the shift from independent toy retailers to mass merchants dated at least to the early '90s.

He would have started stepping up his leadership infrastructure by strengthening his top team. His CFO was already savvy (just ignored and overburdened), so he'd have hired a strong controller to allow the CFO to focus more on strategic plans. He would have also hired a VP of sales and marketing who had worked in retail and wholesale, and who had some toy industry experience as well as experience working for firms selling to mass merchants. So he would have had one strong "inside" executive and one strong "outside" executive. This might have cost $400,000 for the year, reducing pretax profits from $7 million to $6.6 million, assuming there was no upside from the new hires in year one.

These two executives would have been doing some strategic reconnoitering, diligently analyzing the changing marketplace. They, along with the CEO, would have created and agreed to a strategic plan for the company, taking into account all of the realities of the marketplace. A well-informed decision would have already been made about expanding (or not) into the mass market. Let's assume they had decided not to expand to the mass market.

In early 2008 when that bad news came about the customer turned competitor, the strategy team (the owner, the CFO, and the VP of sales and marketing) would have immediately huddled. They would have questioned their assumptions about their strategy and reviewed their strategic plan to see if it should be changed. The CFO, with his strong controller, would have the time to do new financial models looking at acquisitions as a growth strategy. In fact, all three leaders could have carved out most of their time in the following two to four weeks to do a full and rapid strategic review, a thoughtful analysis of how the competitor's actions would play out, and an outline of all the company's options. Thus, they would still be nimble and able to react quickly, but with the higher level of diligence crucial for midsized companies that have so much to lose. (Seven million dollars in annual profits, in this case.)

Even if they'd made the same decisions that the CEO made originally, the CFO would have had the bandwidth to search for and retain a CIO (interim or permanent) to implement the WMS properly. Both the VP of sales and marketing and the CFO would have been part of a proper M&A due diligence effort, surely detecting the flaws in the targeted retail chain.

They would have dodged the killers. This is what will happen when your leadership infrastructure is appropriately developed.

If your leadership infrastructure building goes well, you should see the six following changes as your company grows to the next level:

1. The CEO will become less of a doer and innovator and more of a leader of leaders.
2. The top team's role will change from helping the CEO to leading the business themselves.
3. Midlevel managers will take responsibility for operations, allowing the C-suite to concentrate on long-term strategies.

4. Urgent problems will pop up less often, as their impact will be mitigated by planning and processes.

5. Heroic individual feats of work will no longer be seen (nor will they be necessary) because there will be disciplined teams to handle problems as they emerge.

6. Growth won't depend on opportunities suddenly appearing. It will come by staking out strategic customers and acquisitions.

Sound good? It is good.

Leadership Infrastructure Stabilizes the Company

FIGURE C-2: Leadership infrastructure is like a set of steel beams that stabilizes and helps manage the growth of the business.

Leadership Infrastructure in Action

Pelican Products is a manufacturer of high-performance protective cases and flashlights. For twenty-eight years, the Torrance, California, company expanded through organic growth. But in October 2004, private equity firm Behrman Capital bought out the founder for $200 million. At the time, Pelican had five hundred employees and was generating approximately $100 million in revenues. In August 2006, Lyndon Faulkner came on board to lead the company. Faulkner had been a serial CEO, most recently as general manager of Microsoft's Americas Operations Group.

In September 2008, just as Lehman Brothers filed for bankruptcy and the country teetered at the edge of the abyss that was the Great Recession, Faulkner was negotiating to buy Pelican's arch-competitor, Hardigg Industries, of South Deerfield, Massachusetts, the world's leading manufacturer of high-tech protective cases.

"By then, Pelican had advanced significantly from being a totally entrepreneur-run company to being a more delegated-style company," recalls Faulkner. "We were doing a lot of planning first and execution second, as opposed to the daily execution of a series of tasks. The day-to-day execution style had delivered excellent results in product development over the years, but we had begun to bring strategy to bear in the company. Everybody knew their roles and responsibilities. Many people had been empowered to do more during this period of time than ever before. That, in turn, allowed us to drive growth."

When the $200 million deal to buy Hardigg was announced in January 2009, Pelican suddenly had 1,300 employees and revenues approaching $300 million.

While Hardigg had been successful, it had always been run informally, with little emphasis on planning, project management, and the tight accountability (what I'm calling leadership infrastructure) required of firms that choose to grow aggressively.

"We discovered in the acquisition of Hardigg that they were in the place where Pelican was three years before," Faulkner says. "Hardigg was still a very execution-focused company, not a big analysis company. They made great products and brought them to market. It was what they had decided to do every day and they did it well."

"We went in and, with a clean piece of paper, built a plan around merging the two businesses. A secondary plan was crafted to bring Hardigg's planning and project management acumen up to the place where Pelican was, but in a much shorter time frame."

In short, as its new CEO Faulkner had *grown* leadership infrastructure in Pelican, then *installed* it at Hardigg after the acquisition. Hardigg was now part of a much bigger business and it could no longer simply execute on good ideas; its leadership had to adopt strategy, planning, and governance. And it did. That's mighty.

The Continuing Challenge for the Midsized Business

The years following the Great Recession of 2008 have been difficult for everybody. In essence, the financial meltdown was a giant liquidity crash that engulfed the world, destroying value, killing growth, throwing millions out of work, and bankrupting businesses large, small, and midsized. The economy has bounced back somewhat since then. But employment remains uncomfortably high and the prospects of many midsized companies and industries seem dim.

In fact, most business experts believe there is no going back to the days of economic stability, those times of the 1950s or more recently the late-1990s, when 4 percent annual GDP growth seemed as certain as the next day's sunrise. One of those experts is futurist Bob Johansen of the Institute for the Future, a highly regarded Palo Alto, California, think tank. In 2009, he introduced the acronym VUCA to the business world in his book *Leaders Make the Future*[1]—VUCA stands for volatility, uncertainty, complexity, and ambiguity. Johansen argued that we live in an increasingly VUCA world, and that in that environment specific leadership skills are required to gain competitive advantage.

VUCA particularly affects midsized companies, caught between Fortune 500 companies with enormous financial cushions to withstand unpredictable cash outflows and smaller companies that can stop on a dime to change their offerings as the markets move. The midsized company is, well, caught in the middle of this sea of volatility, and ever more vulnerable to the seven silent growth killers.

Hopefully, they are not so silent now. Perhaps now you'll hear them coming. And before you hear their deadly footfalls, you'll have built the culture, tools, and processes you'll need to deal with them when they appear on your company's doorstep.

"Be prepared" is the Boy Scout's solemn creed. It should be yours, too. The post-2008 economic recovery has been slow. And no matter how high the Dow Jones climbs, businesspeople—especially those running midsized businesses—know that achieving growth in this environment continues to be a challenge. Sometimes, it may even seem impossible.

Despite the world's growing volatility, uncertainty, complexity, and ambiguity, if you can build a mighty midsized company, with the right level of leadership infrastructure, you can position your firm for healthy growth year after year.

And then the growth killers, one through seven or all at once, won't get you.

APPENDIX

Research Background

In December 2011, we began a series of interviews with lead ers of midsized company to explore the factors that facilitate or kill growth. Going into these interviews, I had preliminary thoughts on what those factors were, from years of experience and hundreds of interviews and sessions with midsized CEOs since 2005. But the interviews since 2011 confirmed that some of the growth killers were widespread. In those discussions, I also encountered some new growth killers that I hadn't previously thought to be severe.

Between December 2011 and July 2013, we conducted 101 interviews, many of them recorded and transcribed, in which executives discussed their experiences at 110 companies (listed below). We conducted many (66) interviews in person and the rest by telephone. Some executives spoke to us under the condition of complete anonymity, and are not listed below.

We analyzed and summarized the content of the interviews, and then identified the seven silent growth killers and the approaches to dealing with them. In terms of revenue, we focused on midsized firms, but also talked with some small and large firms, looking for differences in what inhibited or accelerated growth. The distribution of the sample is graphed below.

Companies Researched

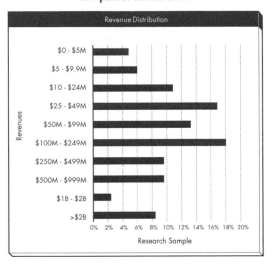

We also report the headcount distribution:

Companies Researched

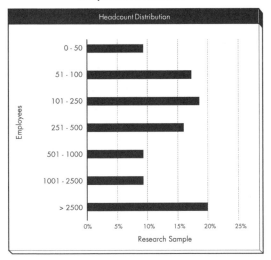

Research Participant Listing

We interviewed the following leaders and we are grateful for the wisdom and time they shared.

Company Name	Leader's Name	Title	Industry
Accenture	John Mack	Managing Director	Management Consulting
ADP Claims Solutions Group	Frank Patchel	Former CFO / COO	Software
Agilent Technologies	Michael Castle	Senior Director of Global Marketing & Strategy - Software & Informatics, Life Sciences Group	Life Sciences
ALOM	Hannah Kain	President and CEO	Logistics
American TonerServ	Andrew Beaurline	Former SVP Corporate Development and Strategy	Printing Supplies and Distribution
Antrim Construction	Jeff Antrim	CEO	Construction
Architectural Glass & Aluminum CA	John Buckley	President	Construction

(Continued)

Company Name	Leader's Name	Title	Industry
Ask Jeeves, Inc.	Marty Reed	Former Director of Finance	Internet Search
Bay View Bank	John Buckley	EVP, Chief Credit Officer	Banking
BlueArc	Rick Martig	Former CFO	Storage
Burr Pilger Mayer Inc.	Steve Mayer	Former CEO	Accounting
Career Choices Inc.	Alex Hehmeyer	Former President and Co-Founder	Proprietary Post-Secondary Education
Caring Senior Service	Jeff Salter	President and CEO	Senior Care
CCC Information Services	Tom Baird	Former SVP Corporate Strategy & Development	Insurance and Automotive Information and Software
Cellairis	Taki Skouras	CEO	Mobile Accessories
Central Garden and Pet	Andrew Beaurline	Former Vice President Corporate Development	Pet and Garden Products Mfg. and Dist.
Chemical Bank	Francine Miltenberger	Former SVP Corporate Merger Office	Financial Services

Cimbal, Inc.	Chris Boone	President and CEO	Mobile Payments
Comstock Mortgage	Craig Sardella	Founder, Business Development Officer	Mortgage
CRC Health Systems	Barry Karlin	Former CEO	Health Care
Cruiser Customizing	Uwe Druckenmueller	Founder and Chairman	Automotive
Dave's Killer Bread	Glenn Dahl	Former CEO	Food & Beverage
Dreamhammer	Nelson Paez	CEO	Software
Ellie Mae, Inc.	Sig Anderman	CEO	Financial Technology
EORM	Glenn Fisher	President and CEO	Environmental, Health, Safety and Sustainability Consulting
Extron	Sandeep Dugal	CEO	Supply Chain/ Last Mile Manufacturing

(Continued)

Company Name	Leader's Name	Title	Industry
Flexstar Technology Inc.	Tony Lavia	Former CEO	Computer Hardware
Food.com	Joan Varonne	Former CFO	Online Recipes & Cooking Tips
Galaxy Desserts	Paul Levitan	CEO	Food
Goddard Systems Inc.	Joe Schumacher	CEO	Education
GoGrid	John Keagy	CEO	Cloud Computing
Goodwill of Silicon Valley	Michael Fox	President and CEO	Non-Profit Institution
Gtronix, Inc.	Hubert Engelbrechten	President	Semiconductor
HeroArts, Inc.	Aaron Leventhal	CEO	Manufacturing-Craft Industry
Huston Patterson Corporation	Thomas Kowa	CEO & Chairman	Printing
IPAC, Inc.	Brian Cereghino	President	Petroleum Additives
Jamba Juice Company	Karen Luey	EVP, CFO & CAO	Restaurant

JetDirect Aviation	Dave Weil	Former Sr. VP of Administration	Aviation Charter
Jones & Stokes	John Cowdery	CEO	Environmental Services
Kaleida Labs, Inc.	Michael Bloom	Director, Business Development	Software
London Bridge Software	Frank Patchel	Former President, RSI Group of London Bridge Software	Software
Look Smart	Dianne Dubois	Former CFO	Internet Search
Mattson Technology	Dave Dutton	Former President and CEO	Semiconductor Equipment
MBH Architects	Dennis Heath	Managing Principal	Architecture
MBH Architects	Oliver Mellows	Principal - Controller	Architecture
MiTAC International Corporation	Angela Liu	Former Director, Corporate Program Management	Electronics
MLS Listings	James Harrison	President and CEO	Software Developer and Real Estate Services
Molecular Devices, LLC	John Senaldi	Former VP/GM	Laboratory Automation

(Continued)

Company Name	Leader's Name	Title	Industry
NetApp	Dan Warmhoven	Former CEO / now Executive Chairman	Computer Storage
Newport Media, Inc.	Sanjay Gokhale	VP Corporate Development	Software-Search
Oclaro, Inc.	Jerry Turin	CFO	Optical Components
Omnicell, Inc.	Nhat Ngo	Executive Vice President	Healthcare Automation
Otis Spunkmeyer Inc.	Robyn Meltzer	Former VP Human Resources	Food Manufacturing
PCM	John Cowdery	COO	Environmental Services
Pelican Products, Inc.	Lyndon Faulkner	CEO	Protective Cases and Advanced Portable Lighting Systems
Performant Financial Corporation	Lisa Im	CEO	Technology Services

PowerTV, Inc.	Michael Bloom	Co-founder, VP, GM, Board Member	Consumer Electronics
Radiance Technologies, Inc.	Tom Engdahl	President & CEO	Internet Acceleration Software
Rambus Inc.	Laura Stark	Senior Vice President, Corporate Strategy, M&A	IP Development
Ramsell Corporation	Eric Flowers	President and CEO	Health Care
Raychem/Thermofit Business Unit	David Ryan	Former CEO	Electronics
Recurve	Andy Leventhal	Former CEO	Software-Construction
Reynolds and Reynolds	Tom Baird	Former VP Corporate Strategy & Development	Software Technology & Printing
Rodan & Fields, LLC	Lori Bush	President and CEO	Consumer Products
SAIC	Mark Iwanowski	Former COO, Telecom and IT Outsourcing Business Unit	Engineering Solutions

(Continued)

Company Name	Leader's Name	Title	Industry
San Francisco Soup Company	Steve Sarver	Owner	Restaurants
Schnader Harrison Segal & Lewis LLP	Kevin Coleman	Partner	Legal Services
SciClone Pharmaceuticals	Friedhelm Blobel	CEO & Member of the Board SciClone Pharmaceuticals, Inc	Pharmaceuticals
Skyline Construction	David Hayes	CEO	Construction
SSA Global Technologies, Inc.	John Walles	EVP	Computer Software
SummerHill Housing Group	Robert Freed	President and CEO	Residential Real Estate Development
Synnex	Angela Liu	Former Director, Business Development	Business Process Services
Takeda San Francisco	Mary Haak-Frendscho	Former President and CSO	Pharmaceuticals
The Colmen Group	Peter Colella	Chairman and CEO	Investment Banking and Turnaround Management and Funding

The Coppola Group of Companies	Calvin Finch	Former VP & CFO	Entertainment, Wine and Hospitality
Torani / R. Torre & Company	Melanie Dulbecco	CEO	Food & Beverage
Total Defense, Inc.	Paul Lipman	CEO	Software-Security
TRC	John Cowcery	Senior Vice President	Environmental Services
Tregaron Capital Company	JR Matthews	Managing Director	Private Equity
TriNet Group, Inc.	Douglas Devlin	Former CFO	HR Services
TRW	Tom Baird	Former Director, Corporate Development	Aerospace, Defense and Automotive Products
United Pacific Forest Products	David Weinstein	President & CEO	Manufacturing Wood Pallets & Crates

(Continued)

Company Name	Leader's Name	Title	Industry
United Site Services	Ken Ansin	Founding Director	Portable Restroom Industry
Various clients	Michael Bloom	Consultant	Hardware, Software, Microelectronics, Consumer Technology
Vivo Pools	Willan Johnson	CEO	Swimming Pool Management
WebMethods, Inc.	Karen McGuire	Former Senior Vice President	Computer Software
Webpass, Inc.	Charles Barr	President	Internet / Telecommunications

We are also grateful to the following individuals who participated in the research: David Chua, Brian Karr, Ken Koenemann, Geraldine Malloy, Joy Montgomery, Navin Nagiah, Greta Remington, Hank Sprintz, R Sundaresen, Amir Talebi, Ken Taylor, and Mark Williamson.

NOTES

Introduction

1 National Center for the Middle Market, The Ohio State University, and GE Capital Corporation, *The Market That Moves America*, October 2011, accessed December 23, 2013, http://www.middle marketcenter.org/middle-market-insights-perspectives-opportunities.

2 Anil Makhija, "Game-Changing Strategies for Superior Growth" (speech delivered on October 30, 2013, at the National Middle Market Summit), accessed December 24, 2013, http://www.middlemar-ketcenter.org/game-changing-strategies-for-superior-growth.

3 President Barack Obama, White House conference call, accessed December 24, 2013, http://www.whitehouse.gov/the-press-office/president-obama-announces-new-small-business-lending-initiatives.

4 *The Market That Moves America.*

5 "Mid-Sized Companies Potentially Responsible for 70% of US Job Growth in 2013," Premium Staffing Inc., accessed December 24, 2013, http://www.premiumstaffinginc.com/2013/10/22/mid-sized-companies-potentially-responsible-70-u-s-job-growth-2013/.

6 Robert Sher, *The Feel of the Deal: How I Built a Company Through Acquisitions* (1 to Ponder, 2007).

Chapter 3

1 National Center for the Middle Market, *3Q 2013 Middle Market Indicator,* accessed December 24, 2013, http://www.middlemar ketcenter.org/3q-2013-middle-market-indicator.

Chapter 4

1 Paul A. Pautler, *The Effects of Mergers and Post-Merger Integration: A Review of Business Consulting Literature* (Bureau of Economics, Federal Trade Commission, 2003), accessed December 26,

2013, http://web.archive.org/web/20041031005622/http://www3.ftc.
gov/be/rt/businesreviewpaper.pdf.

2 Robert Sher, *The Feel of the Deal: How I Built a Company Through
Acquisitions* (1 to Ponder, 2007).

3 KPMG and Steven Kaplan, *The Determinants of M&A Success,*
accessed December 26, 2013, http://www.kpmg.com/NZ/en/Issues
AndInsights/ArticlesPublications/Documents/Determinants-of
-MandA-Success-report.pdf.

Chapter 5

1 Somini Sengupta, Nicole Perlroth, and Jenna Wortham, "Behind
Instagram Feat, Networking the Old Way," *New York Times*
(April 14, 2012), accessed December 26, 2013, http://www.nytimes
.com/2012/04/14/technology/instagram-founders-were-helped-by
-bay-area-connections.html?_r=0.

Chapter 6

1 Robert Half, *Interim Healthcare Business Turnaround Case Study,*
July 2012.

2 CFO Research Services and Expense Reduction Analysts, *The
Path to Prosperity: CFOs at Small and Midsized Companies on
Post-Downturn Cost Control* (June 15, 2011) CFO.com, accessed
December 26, 2013, http://www.cfo.com/research/index.cfm/down-
load/14582386.

Chapter 7

1 Jack and Suzy Welch, "The Loyalty Fallacy," *Businessweek* (January 6, 2009) accessed February 20, 2014, http://www.businessweek
.com/stories/2009-01-06/the-loyalty-fallacy.

2 Jim Collins, *Good to Great: Why Some Companies Make the
Leap...and Others Don't* (New York City: Harper Business,
2001), 20. The book describes a Level 4 leader as "Catalyzes commitment to and vigorous pursuit of a clear and compelling vision,
stimulating higher performance standards."

Conclusion

1 Bob Johansen, Leaders Make the Future: Ten New Leadership
Skills for an Uncertain World (San Francisco: Berrett-Koehler Publishers, 2009), 1-8

REFERENCES

Ansin, Ken. Interview by author. Telephone. January 10, 2012.

Baird, Tom. Interview by author. Telephone. April 20, 2012.

Bush, Lori. Interview by author. In person. San Francisco. February 13, 2013.

CFO Research Services and Expense Reduction Analysts. *The Path to Prosperity: CFOs at Small and Midsized Companies on Post-Downturn Cost Control.* CFO.com (June 15, 2011)

Collins, Jim *Good to Great: Why Some Companies Make the Leap… and Others Don't.* New York City: Harper Business, 2001.

Dahl, Glen. Interview by author. Telephone. March 11, 2013.

Devlin, Doug. Interview by author. In person. San Leandro, Calif. April 5, 2012.

Druckenmueller, Uwe. Interview by author. In person. Livermore, CA. March 13, 2007.

Dulbecco, Melanie. Interview by author. In person. San Bruno, CA. May 31, 2011.

Faulkner, Lyndon. Interview by author. Telephone. September 14, 2012.

Fishler, Glenn. Interview by author. In person. San Jose, CA. June 5, 2012.

Heath, Dennis, John McNulty and Oliver Mellows. Interview by author. In person. Alameda, CA. March 5, 2013.

Johansen, Bob. *Leaders Make the Future: Ten New Leadership Skills for an Uncertain World.* San Francisco: Berrett-Koehler Publishers, 2009.

Karlin, Barry. Interview by author. In person. Menlo Park, CA. April 25, 2012.

Keagy, John. Interview by author. In person. San Francisco, CA. November 7, 2013.

KPMG and Steven Kaplan. *The Determinants of M&A Success.* January 2010.

Levitan, Paul. Interview by author. In person. Richmond, CA. August 18, 2008.

Luey, Karen. Interview by author. In person. Emeryville, CA. February 7, 2012.

Makhija, Anil. "Game-Changing Strategies for Superior Growth." speech delivered at the National Middle Market Summit, October 30, 2013. Accessed December 24, 2013. http://www.middlemarket center.org/game-changing-strategies-for-superior-growth.

Martig, Rick. Interview by author. In person. Santa Clara, CA. May 24, 2012.

Meikle, Paul. Interview by author. Telephone. April 2, 2013.

National Center for the Middle Market, *3Q 2013 Middle Market Indicator.* October 15, 2013. accessed December 24, 2013. http://www. middlemarketcenter.org/3q-2013-middle-market-indicator.

National Center for the Middle Market, The Ohio State University, and GE Capital Corporation. *The Market That Moves America.* October 2011.

Obama, Barack, White House conference call (prior to 2010). Accessed December 24, 2013. http://www.whitehouse.gov/the-press-office/ president-obama-announces-new-small-business-lending-initiatives.

Pautler, Paul A. *The Effects of Mergers and Post-Merger Integration: A Review of Business Consulting Literature* (Bureau of Economics, Federal Trade Commission, 2003). Accessed December 26, 2013. http://web.archive.org/web/20041031005622/http://www3.ftc. gov/be/rt/businesreviewpaper.pdf.

Premium Staffing, Inc. "Mid-Sized Companies Potentially Responsible for 70% of US Job Growth in 2013." Accessed December 24, 2013. http://www.premiumstaffinginc.com/2013/10/22/mid-sizedcom panies-potentially-responsible-70-u-s-job-growth-2013/.

Robert Half. *Interim Healthcare Business Turnaround Case Study.* July 2012.

Schumacher, Joe. Interview by author. Telephone. June 21, 2013.

Sengupta, Somini, Nicole Perlroth and Jenna Wortham. "Behind Instagram Feat, Networking the Old Way." (*New York Times* 14, 2012).

Sher, Robert. *The Feel of the Deal: How I Built a Company Through Acquisitions.* 1 to Ponder, 2007.

Skouras, Taki. Interview by author. Telephone. January 31, 2013.

Taylor, Ken. Interview by author. Telephone. October 14, 2013.

Warmenhoven, Dan. "Leadership Lessons from NetApp." Alliance of Chief Executives, Santa Clara, CA. September 2, 2005.

Welch, Jack and Suzy. "The Loyalty Fallacy." *Businessweek* (January 6, 2009).

Weld, John. Interview by author. Telephone. April 7, 2012.

INDEX

ABOUT THE AUTHOR

Robert Sher is founding principal of CEO to CEO, a consulting firm of former chief executives that accelerates the performance of midsized companies by improving their leadership infrastructure. Based in San Ramon, California, CEO to CEO has worked with the executive teams at more than seventy companies across the U.S., including skincare products seller Rodan + Fields, mobile phone accessories retailer Cellairis, law firm Hanson Bridgett, and cloud services provider GoGrid.

Robert has been published in the *Harvard Business Review, Forbes, CFO* and other leading publications. He is a regular columnist on *Forbes.com* and *CFO.com*, and published a multipart series on HBR.org. He published his first book in 2007, *The Feel of the Deal: How I Built a Company through Acquisitions* (1toPonder). He also publishes his own newsletter, *The CEO Insomnia Factor. Mighty Midsized Companies: How Leaders Overcome 7 Silent Growth Killers* is his second book. He also speaks frequently on the successful leadership traits and skills of CEOs of midsized companies.

Prior to launching CEO to CEO in 2007, Robert was chief executive and co-founder of Bentley Publishing Group from 1984 to 2006. He steered the firm to become a leading player in its industry (decorative art publishing).Early in the business, he and his partners identified a gap in the fast-growing market for framed artwork: high-quality yet affordable prints perfect for the decorative market. Sher and his partners bootstrapped the business, but key successes breathed new life and cash flow into the business. He led the acquisitions of four competitors between 1999 and 2004 and left Bentley two years later. The firm merged with Global Arts in 2011 to form Bentley Global Art Group.

Robert is involved in three Northern California associations for midsized businesses. He has been a director of the Alliance of Chief Executives since 2007; president and board member of the Association for Corporate Growth San Francisco; and an Advisory Board member of the California Israeli Chamber of Commerce.

Robert received a B.S. degree in business administration from Hayward State University in 1986 (during which he ran a small business), and an MBA degree from St. Mary's College in 1988, where he was the recipient of the Jack Saloma Award for student citizenship. From 1995 to 2000, he taught MBA and executive MBA courses at St. Mary's on growing entrepreneurial businesses.

Robert and his wife Renee have two children, Ben and Jessie, and live in Northern California. They love sailing and travel.